I Sense:

At Play in the Field of Healing

Dear Karen:
I hope this book helps
open your 3RD Eye
vision. Love,
Sam

DR. SAMUEL A. BERNE
COLOR STONE PRESS
TESUQUE, NEW MEXICO

DISCLAIMER

This book is not intended to diagnose, treat, or prescribe.
The information contained herein is in no way a substitute
for your own intuition or consultation with a duly licensed
health care-professional.

FIRST EDITION

Manufactured in the United States of America
Cover design by Francene Hart
www.francenehart.com
Text design by Marc Borzelleca

Color Stone Press
Box 458
Tesuque, NM, 87574
www.DrSamBerne.com

CONTENTS

ACKNOWLEDGMENTS

There have been many people who have influenced and helped me with the writing of this book. I'd like to express my gratitude to the teachers who have given me the inspiration to express myself. Albert Shankman, Ellis Edelman, Albert A. Sutton, Dr. E.S.Edelman, Marc Grossman, Konstantin Korotkov, Mary Milroy, Joshua Townsend, Sharin Alpert, Marc Borzelleca, the Esalen Institute, Tom Brady, my African drum circles, Gerald J. and Georgeanne Jud, Hazel Parcells, Emilie Conrad, the Continuum teacher community, Barry Kapp, Cynthia Olivera de Kapp, Audre Gutierrez, the Wisdom of the Earth community, Susan Switzer, the Hawaiian Islands, Wildquest, and the spinner dolphins.

I want to express my deep gratitude to my life partner Charly for her unending devotion to my explorations. And to Magic – the land dolphin!

I SENSE: AT PLAY IN THE FIELD OF HEALING

PREFACE

Disease is often a great teacher. Receiving any medical diagnosis can be harrowing, and our response to this kind of news is determined by our attitudes and experiences. Depending on our context, we might shrivel up – or we might play with the edge and learn from it.

Over the years, I have looked at various healing modalities through this lens: How can we live our lives so we can thrive? Many of us have come to believe that surviving is the most we can hope for, but we can do better than that – we can thrive. Survive or thrive? Your choice...

A second question I play with is how to help people become more responsive to their bodies, because the more aware we are of our physical selves, the more connected we can be to key elements necessary for healthy information flow and vitality. Most of us have "dead zones" in our bodies that we are not even aware of. Let's take an example: your eyes. Many of the eye diseases I have diagnosed over the years are due to nothing more than tissue starvation. We are starving ourselves and we don't even know it!

When they learned I was writing this book, many of my patients asked if I would share my most current strategies. How, they wanted to know, do I get such great results? It's no secret. I have learned how to help people connect with their own healing abilities, using the eyes as an entry point for wellness. This helps people to better access their own energy – which is, after all, free energy.

I also create space for people to come together for healing, as people in a group create a unified field, readily sharing energy with each other and amplifying healing for all members. At workshops or retreats, in a safe, trusting environment, group members can begin to discover their own wellness potential and learn the self-responsibility and self-regulation they need to sustain their health practices. Whether working individually or collectively, as they move into in these practices most people experience a high degree of self-renewal and increased creativity, vitality, and self-love.

I am a pioneer in facilitating this energy field. I believe that I have had many incarnations as a healer, educator, and facilitator, always with the eye-brain-body portal as my starting point.

My patients have followed my exploits as I delved into a variety of disciplines, including Craniosacral therapy, Continuum Movement, dolphin swims, energy field measurements using the GDV camera, and medicinal essential oils. Many of my patients have been my research subjects, allowing me to experiment (successfully!) with them. As I have climbed new mountains, they have joined me.

In this book, I have tried to weave these diverse areas of study and research together like a tapestry, synthesizing my experiences and findings for others – and myself. The completion of this book is my pause to sit at the summit and enjoy the view. I have no idea what the ripple effects will be for you, but if you receive new impulses as you read, try to follow them in the moment, and then ask yourself, "What is next for me?" Keep inquiring! The field is fertile, and your own innovations are waiting to be born.

INTRODUCTION

He Saw an Eagle – A Quest for Vision
Written by Elizabeth Rose, partner of David Burke

Arriving at the Vision Doctor's the first time, David stumbled on the loose stone pathway leading to the geodesic dome that served as his office. His world hazy, peering through prescription triple lenses, David tripped on the unseen step, and arms extended felt his way inside. Guiding his hands, I helped him locate his seat.

Six visits later, David walked unaided, stepping confidently up the path and step, walked directly to his chair, and responded verbally to questions without prompt. Re-doing the same task he attempted two months earlier, the first sheet displayed barely discernible pencil scratchings, the second, bold almost perfect converging lines. A miracle had occurred. Clearly, but what? But how?

Over two years or more his visual symptoms worsened, forcing him to face the truth – he couldn't see. Unable to find the table edge, glass and crockery crashed to the floor splattering wine, tea, coffee, water, juice – his clothes, the floor, wall and upholstery, messed. He stabbed the table missing the food on his plate. He fumbled searching for his knife and fork. "Step ahead. Watch out – pavement." "Watch out – stool." Despite warning cries, he tripped. Paying bills, he either added extra zeros or scrawled illegibly. No longer able to negotiate buttons on the TV remote, he sat before a blank or unselected screen. Phoning became an exasperating experience of misdialed numbers and bleeps.

"I might as well cancel my New Yorker subscription," he announced one day. His G.P. certified him eligible for audio books for the blind. He handed me his car keys.

Autonomy impossible, life as he knew it crumbled. "I am a blind man." David shook his head, defeated.

Opticians, doctors, neurologists and therapists alike suggested yet stronger prescriptions, alternative prisms, Botox injections in the eyelids, sagely agreeing vision problems were to be expected of people suffering from "Parkinson's." "Neurological. Brain. Compromised by the surgical implants," they finalized, avoiding the issue.

"Dr. Samuel Berne," an in-hospital physiotherapist recommended. We "Googled" his name and watched an interview on YouTube. He looked respectable, sounded interesting. "Let's at least give the guy a go," we decided.

"Come in," a gentle voice called. Soft music played. The room, the barefoot doctor welcomed. "Tell me, why you are here?" he asked, attentive.

Finally, someone willing to listen? Hesitant, David looked over, wanting me to be his spokesperson, nodding as I listed his woes.

"Try these and tell me what you see." Doctor B. pointed to an electric-lit eye chart. From behind David's back Doctor B. shook his head as David stood silent, staring blankly at the letters. "Do you mind?" Doctor B. enquired, replacing my husband's prescription progressive triple lenses with a pair of single lenses. "And now?"

"C-F-E-V-M....." David read aloud words from a page of large print. Just like that.

"Single magnification lenses make it easier for the brain/eye to adjust. Triple lenses...on top of that different prescriptions for each eye...the poor brain doesn't know to which depth of field to adjust focus."

Doctor B. believed in re-education of the brain and eye muscles, not their adaptation to ever more complicated prescriptions. How a person sees influences how they navigate the world.

So simple a concept, his ideas made total sense. Doubt melting, David and I looked at each other. We agreed to a block of six biweekly sessions. We both committed to cooperate, even to those exercises far beyond our comprehension and seemingly nothing to do with eyes.

Our attitude: Trust Doctor Berne's wisdom. Accept we know that we don't know what he knows – recognize he is the expert with knowledge of which we are ignorant and may never fully understand – take a leap of faith. His goal sounded logical – to re-awake the body's own bio-intelligence.

Doctor Berne showed us what exercises he wanted us to work on. Homework. I scribbled notes. We had two weeks.

Feeling foolish at first, we hummed, made faces, moved our limbs, lips and pointed and spread our tongue. "To stimulate energy meridians and ventricles in the brain." The retina, he explained, was part of the brain.

Rotating single magnification lenses – 300 for distance, 400 for closer, mid range, and the 500 – on, off, taped, untapped, with eye patches, and without, David squinted down his nose along a length of string struggling to focus on spaced colored beads to strengthen eye muscles.

Peering at print through black, pin-holed lenses, we discovered the letters jumped suddenly into focus after a few seconds and we could read.

Picking out letters and symbols from charts to develop visual discrimination and tracking, we were kids at kindergarten all over again. Seemingly such a simple task, it took a great effort of concentration.

David relaxed beneath a blue gel visor watching TV. "Just encouraging my peripheral vision," he smiled.

To build brain-hand-eye coordination, develop both visual and auditory comprehension and build memory, we confused our brains with mind-gym games. One 4-level task involved pointing to a chart of directional arrows: up down left right. Instructions: Do and say the same. Do and say the opposite. Do the same, say the opposite. Say the same, do the opposite. Level 3 and 4 still twist our brains to knots.

"Catch." I threw a ball at David. "Catch." He threw it back. Our living room became a playground of bouncing balls, the beat of a metronome, card games and floating juggling scarves. Simultaneously calling out letters from charts and newspaper headlines, we wobbled heel-toe walking straight along the join lines of our floor tiles.

Poor performance didn't matter so much as attempting the tasks. But David lacked motivation. Doing them each day was an issue.

"Ah. I was waiting for you to bring that up....," Doctor B. said on the fifth session. "From the time we first met, it was apparent David's life-force was severely depleted, but it was important for you to have that realization before addressing the problem." So to oxygenate and re-vitalize his body, breathing exercises, dietary changes, supplements, essential oils were prescribed. To reduce toxins in the body, we both gave up sleeping pills.

Strange, even weird though some exercises seemed, Doctor B. made them less so by explaining their purpose. Most tasks were fun. We practiced most of what he showed as regularly as we were able.

By increments David's body/mind/eye skills improved. His voice strengthened. The most striking – David began initiating many exercises himself. Relieved of my therapist role, I could step back. David's old self, my companion, husband glimmered. Hope returned.

One afternoon six or seven weeks into Doctor B.'s sessions, we were visiting friends in Colorado, when David gave a shout.

"Hey. I can read," and reeled off sentences from the book on his lap, his face shining. In disbelief, as though to prove it to himself, he read out paragraph after paragraph. "I might paint, I might even drive again," he added.

A friend remarked, "Staggering change – David's agility compared to six months ago." Our neighbor told of watching David's daily driveway walk to the mailbox. No stick, not stumbling, David walks balanced, unaided, stepping long and swinging his arms, an apple in his hand to offer to the neighbor's horse.

Demonstrating getting up and down from a low chair at the neurologist's office, she exclaimed, "You don't present as a Parkinson's patient today. Keep on with whatever it is you are doing. It's working."

"We have the Vision Doctor to thank for that," we told her and described some of the therapy.

"You've taught me something today," she said writing down his name.

It's not to say David is without disability. The Parkinson-related problems will never be gone. Some days are depressingly bad. When he is tired, his voice fades. He lolls tilted sideways in his chair, gazes at the flickering television screen for hour upon hour, and finds it difficult to initiate verbal response. He muddles which pair of glasses is appropriate to specific tasks. He is frustrated with himself – his continuing difficulties, the slow grind of his progress.

Good days, he reads newspaper articles and a page or two from a book, sometimes completes "find-the-word" games, calls out passing road signs from the car's passenger seat, picks out landscape details and antelope hitherto unseen, practices breathing/ humming, is motivated to do daily exercises. David's next goal – rebuild computer and typing skills.

Last week we drove to the Bosque Del Apache wetlands. The sun shone. As we entered the sanctuary several hundred migrating snow geese rose from the lake and circled low. Back and over, around and around, they dipped and glided above the water again and again. Leaning backwards across the car's hood as the massive flock passed overhead, so low, David picked out their yellow feet tucked beneath the whiteness of their wings, a white made more brilliant by the blueness of the cloudless sky.

Continuing our drive through the wetlands, David spotted groups of grazing sand cranes. We parked and exited the car and watched them feeding in the grass. "Did you see that?" David remarked, his eyes glued. "One leaped into the air with a flap of its grey wings."

Farther along we stopped at an observation deck. The sights of the park's mounted binoculars pointed across the water trained on the skeleton of a lone tree. With my naked eye I could pick out a large bird – its white cowl and trouser legs, yellow feet, yellow beak. I watched its head face back then front. Using his 300 magnification pair of glasses, David located the tree. It's been years since he has been able to use binoculars. He pressed close to the binocular eye-piece.

"An eagle. I can see an eagle."

I SENSE: AT PLAY IN THE FIELD OF HEALING

CHAPTER ONE

BEHIND OUR EYES

— *How do you feel about your eyesight?*
— *Do you see things clearly?*
— *Are you frustrated that your eyes get worse as you get older?*
— *Does your eye doctor increase your prescription every year?*
— *How do you feel about your blur?*
— *Does anyone in your family have the big three: macular degeneration, glaucoma, or cataracts?*
— *And here is the elephant in the room: Are you afraid of going blind? For many of us, blindness is a core unspoken fear always at the back of our minds.*

❖ ❖ ❖ ❖ ❖ ❖ ❖

Over the years, many people have asked me to describe my work. I usually begin by saying that early in my career, after earning my Doctorate in Optometry, I found a niche as a Behavioral Optometrist. This holistic specialty uses a series of techniques and eye-brain activities to improve eyesight and visual processing in both children and adults. Soon, I began using the eyes as an entry point for improving overall health and, eventually, developed a unique approach to vision and wellness.

Early in my career I had three major experiences that were formative in my evolution.

First, after completing my optometry training, I enrolled at the Gesell Institute, a post-doctoral training that promotes deeper understanding of child development. There, I learned to evaluate children's learning styles from a developmental perspective, focusing on ways to improve sensory-motor functioning in children who had developmental delays.

One of the most important things I learned at the Gesell Institute is to look beyond the symptom to find a root cause. For example, if the symptom is blurred distance vision (a child has difficulty seeing the blackboard), the root of the problem may be that the child's eyes do not track or coordinate together at close range. I learned that if we treat the near-point stress, many times distance acuity then returns to normal. In fact, over 30% of vision problems in children are missed because the distance chart, the standard measurement for most eye doctors, does not uncover these problems. (Since my time there, I have counseled school nurses to screen children with a near visual chart instead of relying on a distance chart. They have told me that children's facial expressions while reading the near visual chart are often enough to indicate that the problem is in the child's near vision.)

Taking this further, the Gesell Institute taught me that vision problems do not reside exclusively in the eyes. It isn't correct or helpful to blame poor vision on a defective eyeball because the roots of visual symptoms are systemic. If our eyes are letting us down, it is almost always because of the programming behind the eyes. We need to look deeper, starting with movement habits, posture, emotional responses, and biochemistry.

This led me to a realization: Vision is a pattern that reflects the scroll of our life history. Most eyeglass or contact lens prescriptions are just printouts of the programming our brains and bodies have experienced up to the moment when the prescription was written. The lens you receive represents your programming, not the reality of your eyes. And, because lenses prescribed to correct distance blur represent a symptom-based approach that fails to look at the reasons behind the symptoms, they weaken your vision even more.

What, then, is seeing clearly? I say it is not just about what we see outside ourselves, but also how clearly we see from our inside vision, our inner vision. I call it learning to see from the inside out. Seeing clearly on the outside is a by-product of how clearly we see on the inside.

Another vital thing I learned at the Gesell Institute is that, as the embryo develops during gestation, the eyes grow out of brain tissue. That means that when I help people with their eyes, I am actually working with their brains. Often, when we become more aware of our eyes, we begin to uncover some of our birth imprints, including our relationship with gravity, our breathing pattern, and our ability bond and attach to others. We also lay down the foundation for the ways we engage socially.

❖ ❖ ❖ ❖ ❖ ❖ ❖

The second important milestone in my early training was discovering ways to treat people suffering from unusual eye problems. After completing my training at Gesell, I associated with holistic optometrist, Dr. Ellis Edelman. I had a hard time attracting patients in this conservative, medically-oriented area, so I began to use my vision techniques at a hospital's out-patient rehabilitation center. I worked with patients who the regular eye doctors had given up on, traumatic brain injury and stroke survivors who had balance problems, double vision, and memory loss. Using physical therapy techniques that I learned from Dr. Edelman for the eyes and brain, I helped these people rehabilitate their vision within 3-6 months of receiving their diagnosis. I got rave reviews and felt like a rock star! The results were so great that I started consulting with several hospitals in the area and began to build my private practice. By helping people in an innovative way, I was filling an unmet need.

I also began using the same rehabilitative, physical eye-therapy techniques with special needs children who had conditions like minimal brain dysfunction, cerebral palsy, and autism. To everyone's amazement, these children's development and learning improved as they began seeing better. I was curious about how these children saw the world and they became my teachers as I began a serious inquiry into how to help them.

❖ ❖ ❖ ❖ ❖ ❖ ❖

My third significant experience was meeting a doctor who helped me heal my own visual disability. I had a visual coordination problem coupled with moderate myopia with astigmatism and needed lenses to see anything! Dr. Albert Shankman, a developmental optometrist, was a very spiritual man, a practicing yogi who was in his mid-70s when we met. He became one of my mentors, teaching me through his techniques that seeing is very much a whole body experience.

❖ ❖ ❖ ❖ ❖ ❖ ❖

I began developing myopia, astigmatism, and reading and learning problems when I was eight years old. It was a time when my world was out of control. I had just started a new school, was having a hard time with reading, and my parents' marriage was falling apart. I was a sensitive child. There was nothing and no one I could trust. I did not have the resources to deal with what was happening to me.

Looking back, it's not surprising that I developed vision problems at such an overwhelming time in my young life. Here's how I interpret it now: I was afraid and anxious and didn't know how to make sense of my outer world, so part of my brain decided to take control by pulling my vision inward, internalizing my trauma into my eyes and my body. This allowed me to feel more control in my world, to manage at least part of my experience, to protect myself in some way, and to numb my feelings. Pulling my visual world inward allowed me to live, even if it was in survival mode. Although I lost some of my distance sight, this adaptation allowed me to honor my sensitivity. Years later when I started to practice Craniosacral therapy, and teach Continuum Movement, I began to broaden the way I defined myself. Instead of identifying with my past, I began to connect with a broader species inclusive consciousness. This new awareness freed me from being re-stimulated by my historical data. Not only was I relatives with my mammalian friends, I also had connections with my reptilian ancestors.

❖ ❖ ❖ ❖ ❖ ❖ ❖

Practitioners and teachers in the field of Continuum Movement will tell you that we have some unlikely relatives. Our development includes contributions from species that seem as different from us as night from day.

One important part of our genetic legacy is the "reptilian response" or survival response– a response to perceived threats that originates in a part of the brain that first developed in reptiles early in our evolution. When the reptilian brain is dominant, our nervous system becomes hyper-vigilant, reacting with a "fight, fight, or freeze" response even in situations that may not be truly dangerous.

We all first experience this survival response in utero or during birth through a primitive reflex called the Moro reflex. It is part of the "startle response," the Moro reflex is a movement pattern infants use to adjust to new surroundings. It might also be triggered in utero if the mother is ill, needs bed rest, uses harsh medications, is exposed to toxicities, or experiences strong emotions, or during birth, especially if there are any complications. For most babies, the Moro reflex integrates during infancy, but this may not happen if a baby is in distress or does not bond with its parents or caretaker. These reflexes from gestation, birth, and bonding/attachment can set the foundation for our systems to habitually react as though we are experiencing a threat.

Established in our earliest development, a survival response may be triggered by violence or abuse, difficult emotional states, pain, and other stressors. While manifestations like PTSD are most well known, the survival response can manifest in any system of the body, including the eyes.

❖ ❖ ❖ ❖ ❖ ❖ ❖

I was taken to an eye doctor, who gave me my first prescription. This first lens he prescribed further validated and embedded my own traumatic programming.

During my adolescence, I continued to experience chaos in the family. To get away from this intensity, I retreated into my thoughts and my studies. As a way to survive, I became an obedient robot.

Every year I would go to the eye doctor to get a stronger

lens. Many of the activities I gravitated to during this time, like running, biking, and lifting weights, involved repetitive physical movements which contributed to a mind-body experience of isolation, numbness, compression. I also began questioning my family's religious traditions. This religious conditioning also became internalized in my eyes and my body. Not only did my eyes become steadily worse throughout my adolescence, my body became extremely armored.

❖ ❖ ❖ ❖ ❖ ❖ ❖

When I was taught the allopathic model of eye care in optometry school, it reminded me of all the other indoctrinations I had been expected to adopt throughout my life. I began to question all of my history. Feeling new energy rise up in me, I began searching.

After I graduated from Optometry school, I started working with Dr. Shankman, who helped me develop a system to improve my own vision. With his guidance, I was able to let go of many of the perceptions I carried in my eyes, especially those that grew from conditioned survival response patterns, and this finally allowed me to begin to come out of the maximum security prison created by my childhood.

Within two years I completely reversed my myopia. My eyesight improved to 20/20, with no need for any lenses. To this day, I don't need a lens to see clearly. But more important than reducing the prescription, the mind-body healing I experienced taught me that vision is more than an eyeball experience. It taught me that we are all programmed by spoken and unspoken messages imparted by our families, cultures, religions, education, health care, and government. Once I realized how hard it is to even notice this subtle programming, the revolutionary part of me begin to boil up and I decided that my path would be to continue to help people, including myself, to find choices in our own evolution. My approach would be to use the eyes as the entry point to heal vision problems and teach people to use the process as a self-inquiry.

❖ ❖ ❖ ❖ ❖ ❖ ❖

First eye opener: Any prescription measured in the eyes exists also in the body. It can be found in our posture, movement, thinking, emotional-psychological reactions, and energy.

❖ ❖ ❖ ❖ ❖ ❖ ❖ ❖

Try looking through your vision instead of looking at the world. When we look at something, our survival response kicks in and we tighten our eyes as a way to feel in control. Can you begin to feel what this means?

❖ ❖ ❖ ❖ ❖ ❖ ❖ ❖

Many of the problems we have with our vision are a result of how much effort we put into "keeping it together." This pattern is exhausting for our eyes. If only we could allow our eyes to be a little out of control...

❖ ❖ ❖ ❖ ❖ ❖ ❖ ❖

In addition people tend to have a confuse their visual midline and their body midline. Many of us favor one eye over the other, to the point that one of our eyes is suppressed, left behind so to speak. When this occurs, it affects what we call "depth perception," and it also affects how deeply we can see into the world and into ourselves. When parts of our vision are suppressed so that we are unable to see the whole picture, we may begin to let our proprioception override our vision. Part of what I teach is to feel into our eyes and our eye sockets, because the more we connect to our eyes on a feeling level, the more we can truly see.

❖ ❖ ❖ ❖ ❖ ❖ ❖ ❖

Here's another piece of the puzzle: Although our eyes and brain only make up 2% of our body weight, they require 25% of our food intake to thrive. Most people's eyes are undernourished, dehydrated, and poorly oxygenated, primarily because of traumas, stress, and toxicities throughout our eyes, brain, and body.

❖ ❖ ❖ ❖ ❖ ❖ ❖

When I first started using modalities like Craniosacral therapy, I saw striking changes in people after their sessions. They could read the eye chart much more clearly and said the lenses they were using felt too strong. This led me to talk more with patients about sensing and feeling into their eye tissues.

Not many of us have thought about the connections between our mouths and our eyes. When I ask patients to place their tongues at the roof of the mouth and press into the soft palate, within a minute or less, they report that they can feel their eyes relaxing. Yes, the tension we carry in our teeth, jaw, mouth, and face has a profound effect on the tension we carry in our eyes. In fact some somatic therapists say that, because our vision is both our most dominant sense and a holding place for our survival responses, between 60-80% of body tension is carried in the eyes. There are consequences when our eyes become a dumping ground for our tensions and fears.

- For one, we lose the ability to feel the eyes. I know this because as soon as I began to use a lower prescription and move my eyes slowly and more regularly, I became able to sense the tightness I held in my eyes. It dawned on me that this was a way I'd protected myself from the world.

- For another, we start to tunnel our vision. We exclude our peripheral vision and only look at things straight ahead. We hold our breath and tighten our body. It is a classic survival, reptilian response to perceived threat.

- Most important is recognizing that this is how the deterioration of our vision begins.

The more connection we feel with the inside of our eyes, the more connected we will be to our environment and the more solid we will feel moving our bodies through space. Our relationship with nature will deepen, causing our fluid bodies and nervous systems to slow down. And we will start to become able to truly sustain our own wellness.

❖ ❖ ❖ ❖ ❖ ❖ ❖

The more spontaneous and slowly we move our eyes, the better we will see. The more we feel into our eyes, the better we will see. The deeper our intuitions and sensations into our eyes, the more clearly our externalizations will be recognized. Our vision then will flourish. Our creativity will soar!

I SENSE: AT PLAY IN THE FIELD OF HEALING

CHAPTER TWO

CHANGING FILTERS ABOUT OUR EYES: TRUTHS VERSUS MYTHS

The eyes are organs of light comprising almost 130 million photoreceptors, with connections to our endocrine and nervous systems and to acupuncture meridians, chakras, and energy fields.

The eyes are portals we can use to achieve expanded consciousness and awareness, both physically and spiritually.

Most of us don't realize that our eyes hold this power. We are taught that the eyes are independent of our other organs, and we expect our eyes, and all parts of our bodies, to deteriorate as we age.

Truths About Our Eyes

Truth: Vision problems offer us an opportunity to rebalance the energetic and systemic health of the whole body.

Truth: Chinese medicine tells us that many major meridians connect to the eyes. Stagnation in the liver, kidney, and spleen meridians can create pain, swelling, and inflammation in the eyes with resulting impaired vision. Acupuncture can reduce the stagnation, decreasing symptoms and re-balancing the eyes.

Truth: We have been conditioned to disconnect from sensing our eyes. As I have helped people discover the sensations in their eyes, they report that their sight is clearer, brighter, and more vibrant.

Truth: Sunlight provides important nourishment for the eyes and is necessary for our systemic and spiritual health. When ultraviolet light enters our eyes, it helps to stimulate vitamin D production and nourish the immune system.

Truth: Vision can be improved at ANY age.

❖ ❖ ❖ ❖ ❖ ❖ ❖

Truth: Children's eye problems don't have a statue of limitations for improvement. Therapies can be organic and holistic and are effective at any time during development. We don't have to rush into surgery, there are complementary alternatives that work!

Neuroscientists have proved that we can improve the function of the brain at any age by developing new neural connections. The brain, the eyes — every part of the body with nerve connections — is capable of lifelong neural flexibility, or neuroplasticity.

Truth: Our vision is not static. It is a dynamic system and should be treated as such. The more versatility we have in our vision, the more versatility we have in our lives.

Different views

The number of people in the general population who have actual eye disease is less than 15%, and yet eye doctors spend 95% of our time looking for disease. Medical schools for eye doctors indoctrinate us to look through one lens only — the lens that is focused on disease.

In our Western culture, most of us have been conditioned to seek the quick fix. Rather than be in the present, we're always a step ahead of ourselves. "Let's get this over with," we seem to say, "so we can move on to the next thing!" As we become increasingly addicted to the speed of our PCs, laptops, tablets, and smart phones, we are forced to disconnect from our own natural rhythms. (And the electromagnetic pollution from these devices doesn't do our energy and health any good, either.)

❖ ❖ ❖ ❖ ❖ ❖ ❖ ❖

A new patient, Mindy ("All patient names have been changed to protect their privacy,") , called after an appointment at the city eye clinic, where she was told she had the very beginnings of cataracts in both eyes. For preventive reasons, the doctor wanted to remove her lenses and insert artificial ones. They assured her this was very minor surgery with a high success rate.

But when I examined Mindy, I couldn't see any need for surgery. The change in her lenses was minimal. Instead I offered her two kinds of homeopathic eye drops to dissolve the cataracts. When Mindy returned less than a month later, the pre-cataract changes in her lenses were gone.

I've noticed a disturbing trend in the education of eye doctors. Each new generation of doctors is trained to be more aggressive in the ways they perceive and treat problems. The result is an increasing number of unnecessary eye procedures. Sadly, these unneeded surgeries can actually weaken the eye structures, making other parts of the eye vulnerable to change. Neil's story offers another example:

Neil scheduled an emergency visit to his eye doctor when he started seeing flashes in his left eye. Fearing a detached retina, the doctor immediately performed laser surgery to isolate the possible detachment.

While the surgery left a blurred spot in his vision from the scar on his retina, Neil got used to it and was relieved to think his possible detachment had been corrected. Eventually, he developed a cataract in the same eye, which is, I have observed a secondary response to the laser surgery, and required a lens replacement. Unfortunately, the lens implant's alignment was off by a microscopic amount, resulting in glare. Now, both blur and glare interfered with the vision in Neil's left eye. The surgeon replaced the misaligned lens, but within a short time a membrane began to grow over the new implant, distorting Neil's vision. Following a procedure to clean up the membrane, Neil developed low tension glaucoma (decreasing pressure in the eye), and his surgeon scheduled yet another procedure, to insert a sclera buckle, or staple, to help the eye maintain its shape and pressure.

This cascading series of procedures left Neil with blurred vision in one eye, an increased risk of requiring further interventions, and a feeling that his vision was permanently disabled. His eyes were always dry from the glaucoma medication, and he was seeing halos around lights.

❖ ❖ ❖ ❖ ❖ ❖ ❖

If Neil had come to me when he started seeing flashes, my response would have been very different. Depending on the results of my examination and his answers to my questions, we might have started with Vision Therapy (a form of physical therapy for the eye-brain connection) to help him broaden his peripheral vision. We would probably have reduced his lens prescription so his eyes were more relaxed, as the more power in the lens, the tighter the eye tissue becomes. Tightness means less energy flow, poor circulation and a starvation of the tissue. We might have used Craniosacral therapy to create more movement in the cranial bones, and possibly medicinal essential oils to help oxygenate the eye tissue. Other possibilities might have included light/color therapy to improve cellular nutrition in the retina and switching to structured water, which has a high photonic energy and is more readily absorbed into the cells helping to improve the hydration of eye tissues and entire the entire body.

Neil's story might sound like a tale of extreme bad luck, but scenarios of this kind are increasingly common. There are times when surgery and pharmaceuticals are warranted and needed, but leaping to these interventions without considering other options is narrow, often ineffective, and sometimes harmful. Patients would be better served if their eye doctors exchanged the lens of looking for eye disease for a new lens, one that sees the whole person, including the systemic and spiritual connection we have with our eyes. Then they might be better able to assist in improving or healing their patients' vision.

There is a reason that this new lens is not being used. Eye

I SENSE: AT PLAY IN THE FIELD OF HEALING

care professionals have been indoctrinated to believe that the eye inevitably deteriorates with age, that it is a purely mechanical structural system, that functional control and change are impossible, and that alternative therapies are useless at best. Sadly, if you have a retina problem, your doctor probably only sees you as two retinas and not as a whole person. If you have a problem in the lens of your eye, he or she sees you as two lenses. Worse yet, children's vision is evaluated in the same manner.

❖ ❖ ❖ ❖ ❖ ❖ ❖

The way children are treated in our medical system is frightening all too often based on myths and outdated information. For example, often a parent may take an infant or toddler to the eye doctor because one of the child's eyes is turning in or out, and the surgeon's response is to insist that the child requires surgery as soon as possible. The surgeon may offer literature that says that if a "lazy eye" isn't repaired by age seven, it never will improve.

These eye doctors are trained to perform surgery. It's the only lens they know how to look through. Parents, I have a different message. Please read this slowly and move your lips:

> **What those doctors are telling you is a MYTH, based on old, outdated information.**

If you look at the literature, this kind of surgery has a low success rate. That's because the brain controls the eyes, and if you try to straighten the eye without reprogramming the brain and body, sooner or later the eye will revert to the way it was before the surgery. This is why multiple surgeries are often "required."

In fact, the child may have crossed eyes due to stress, karma, genetics, toxicity, or an adaptive response to trauma, which manifests in the eyes but actually exists in the person's consciousness. We can learn more from the child's movement, posture, emotional responses, and energy patterns. These children often do well with a re-education movement process, using a developmental lens that involves the eyes-brain-body-spirit. While it might take more time before you see results, they will be much longer lasting.

Another misguided protocol is forcing a child to wear a patch over the so-called stronger eye for eight hours a day to "force" the weak eye to work. This idea is nothing more than cave-man medicine. First of all, I would ask all the eye doctors out there to wear a patch eight hours a day and let me know how YOU feel after a week. No child has the resources to understand why the doctor is recommending this.

Putting aside of the traumatic effects on the children subjected to it, this treatment does not work. The eye patch teaches the eyes that they are separate from the rest of the body. But since the eyes are actually an extension of the brain and bodies, a better approach is to help the child to self-discover: "Look, I have two eyes! Look, they are part of my body!" If we can help children learn how to use their two eyes in the context of connecting to their body through balancing, moving, and thinking, there is a much better chance for both eyes to work together. Again this process may take more time, but it is healing rather than traumatizing, and the results are transformative and long lasting.

❖ ❖ ❖ ❖ ❖ ❖ ❖

Myths about our eyes dominate the thinking of the eye-care profession. Here are a few them:

Myth: The eye is a simple, mechanical/biological organ, separate from the rest of the body which will inevitably deteriorate with age.

Starting with the industrial revolution, we humans, along with our machines, have become increasingly robotic. In more and more areas of our lives, we repeat the same movement patterns – consider computer games and text messages, think about workplace tasks. Our ever-growing use of electronic devices causes visual confinement, so that for large parts of our lives we are living in a two-dimensional world rather than the three-dimensional world our bodies, eyes included, were designed for. Mechanical repetitive movement has also become common in the fitness world, where the price we pay for greater body density and muscle mass is increased rigidity. In fitness, work, or leisure, repetitive movements create closed systems in our bodies, leading to decreased flexibility and increased aging in all realms – moving, seeing, and thinking.

Myth: Our genes control our eye health.

When mainstream medicine tells us that our genes determine our health, it leaves us feeling like victims of our own heredity. While we can't change our genes, we can influence how they are expressed. Scientists like Dr. Bruce Lipton in the new field of epigenetics don't agree that we are simply a product of our genes. Rather, they say, the expression of our genes is a result of the environment surrounding them.

Myth: If you don't wear your glasses, your eyes will get worse.

Glasses and contact lenses keep the eyes stuck in one position. The more we wear lenses, the more embedded the visual system becomes as the lenses reinforce our habitual ways of seeing. Instead of movement, our eyes become paralyzed and can only accommodate to what the lens has to offer.

I once did a research study and found that 95% of all patients were over-correcting their eyes by using prescriptions that were too strong. A prescription is nothing more than a read-out of what your mind-brain tells your eyes; it can reveal a lot about your history and how you have reacted to life situations. In fact, if you look back to the time when you received your first prescription, you may unlock the reasons why you began programming your eyes to see in a distorted manner. Often, it's a survival response from a time when a person did not feel safe in the world.

Myth: There is no correlation between the eyes and the rest of the body.

This myth lives on because we have such a hard time being in touch with our eyes. Most people don't feel their eyes working when they look at something. We have been conditioned to numb our awareness of our eyes because so much emphasis is placed on getting it right and being perfect. The more we live in hyper-vigilance, the more our reptilian brain gets stimulated — triggering our fight, fright, freeze response. Certainly, when danger arises, the reptilian brain helps protect us. However, when we only know the hyper-vigilant state, there is no option to move out of this response.

Myth: Vision loss is caused by defects in our eyeballs.

The eyeballs are not at fault here. It is our mind-brain – the programming behind the eye – that creates changes in the eyeball. When our mind-brain sends a message that the world is too chaotic, it tells our eyes to blur what they are seeing. The eyes believe the mind-brain and, after a while, actually change their shape to accommodate the programming. When our eye doctors describe the problems they perceive with our vision, they validate our mind-brain programming.

Myth: Everyone over age 45 is presbyopic, meaning they have a diminished ability to focus on nearby objects.

We don't have to lose our close-up vision. There are techniques and practices we can use to improve visual flexibility so that magnification lenses are unnecessary. You may notice that the more you wear reading glasses, the less responsive your eyes become when you take them off. That's because the brain immediately notices the artificial magnification and allows the eyes to "go to sleep," and with less movement, the eye muscles begin to atrophy.

❖ ❖ ❖ ❖ ❖ ❖ ❖

Why do we learn so many myths about our eyes and so little truth? In large part, this is due to the state of our health care (or more accurately, disease care) system, which is designed around financial incentives rather than the needs of patients. In this environment, a doctor might hire technicians and invest in expensive technology in order to generate higher insurance reimbursements. That done, paying for the equipment and payroll expenses becomes the office's priority and the doctor must see as many people as possible, rather than spending enough time with each patient to provide high quality care.

I understand this dilemma. I once had nine employees and was so busy that I hired assistants to see my patients. But then I recognized how flawed this model was – my patients weren't satisfied and neither was I. I closed that office and opened a much smaller one, where I made sure there was enough time for each patient.

Doctors, maybe you could shift your focus to seeing their patients as individuals with unique needs and concerns, rather than fitting them all into a pre-formed agenda. Maybe having the largest square footage in your area is less important than deeply seeing and hearing your patients during their appointments. Wouldn't it be great if you could match your treatment protocol to the individual patient's belief system? I think you'd find that you would see more improvement – without the invasiveness and expense of surgery.

❖ ❖ ❖ ❖ ❖ ❖ ❖

Can we change the way people understand vision, moving from a narrow focus on basic biology to a psycho-spiritual recognition of the eye-brain connection? Can we broaden the popular understanding about the way our eyes function to include experience-based insights?

My wish for us all is to be able to accept the possibilities of a larger view…the big picture, expanded vision, learning to experience vision as fresh, in the moment, instead of seeing through the filter of personal history.

❖ ❖ ❖ ❖ ❖ ❖ ❖

The strategies I use for eye health work with three spheres of vision: Traditional, Embryonic, and Universal.

The traditional sphere: This is the world of conditioned responses that we learned or inherited without noticing. We accept them as given and rarely realize that they are optional. When operating in the traditional sphere, we may internalize our visual experiences and store them in our memory banks, and they very quietly influence us without our even knowing it.

Eyes are "pattern addicts." Here are two examples of problematic patterns that can arise from the traditional sphere:

1. We focus our eyes harder in order to "see right."
2. We tunnel our vision, excluding everything outside a narrow focus.

When the normal evolutionary process of development is disrupted, maybe by stress, trauma, or exposure to toxicities, the mind adapts by tapping into a fight or flight response, the brain's most basic defense system. It may then send a message to the eyes telling them to compensate, protect, and withdraw, creating what I call 2-D vision. Computers, tablets, and smart phones all support this kind of visual narrowness.

The embryonic sphere: Like our brain and skin, our eyes are mostly made up of tissue that originated in utero, a direct descendent from our pre-vertebral origins. The embryo's primitive survival reflexes continue to influence eye development during infancy. But these protective reflexes should recede into the background of our brain function by toddler age; when they do not, they can create problems by dominating the overall sensory system every time we perceive a threat in our environment.

Gestation, birth and delivery, bonding and attachment are important preverbal experiences that shape our overall sensory motor development. Because difficult early experiences may create persistent survival reflexes, when children have learning problems or coordination challenges it can be useful to probe their early imprints.

When I start talking about the embryonic sphere in private sessions and workshops, participants often begin connecting to these times in their lives. They connect the threads and begin to understand the effect their survival responses have had on their vision.

Universal seeing: Can we recognize the difference between seeing through a hole and seeing the whole? In the universal sphere we can see both the big picture and the details simultaneously. Our arteries and veins form fractal patterns, connecting us to both the microcosm and macrocosm of the whole: each branch connects us equally to the dendrites in our nerve endings and to the dendrite-shaped fractals we see in distant spiral galaxies. As we connect with these fractals, we become more unified and able to connect to our biocosmic intelligence, which helps nourish and feed us.

Often, I ask people to assess the balance of these three aspects of their seeing, and most people find they exist mostly in the traditional seeing paradigm. But if they are offered alternatives, many become able to move beyond this sphere and broaden their vision.

❖ ❖ ❖ ❖ ❖ ❖ ❖

"Arlene" sought help because of a growing blind spot in her right eye's optic nerve, reducing her ability to see three dimensionally and affecting her balance. Specialists had ruled out glaucoma, MS, and cancer, but remained unable to find the source of her problem or to recommend a treatment.

After examining Arlene and hearing her story, I had a hunch that we should request biochemical testing. When the tests revealed toxic levels of both lead and cadmium in her system, I wasn't surprised. According to Chinese medicine, the liver rules the eyes, and Arlene's liver must have been under great stress from her high levels of toxicity.

Arlene agreed to try four modes of treatment that I suggested. First, I prescribed therapeutic prism glasses in order to create more stimulation for the optic nerve. This immediately improved her balance and allowed her to see in three dimensions again.

We also started a nutritional and aromatherapy program designed to remove the heavy metals from her system while boosting her immunity, and color therapy to help re-sensitize the photo receptors in her retinas.

The last therapy we added, Continuum Movement, became Arlene's favorite. In a daily practice, she employed a special breathing technique while visualizing the ways her visual health and overall well-being were improving. She said she found this protocol particularly calming and rejuvenating.

After following this program for four months, Arlene's visual field was restored. Her visual system and overall health remain robust. To maintain her visual and overall health, she checks in with me every six months and attends one of my intensive retreats yearly. Her home self-care includes Continuum Movement sequences and a variety of medicinal essential oils. Arlene now has a variety of resources to help her maintain her vision.

Remember: When we connect to our own biology for wellness, our eyes have the ability to heal!

❖ ❖ ❖ ❖ ❖ ❖ ❖

It's unusual for eye doctors to think outside the allopathic box. I guess I'm unique – I can't think inside of it. I am constantly probing and asking questions, like:

What are our eyes really saying?

How can we let go of "looking at" from the front part of our eyes, and instead use our eyes to see from the visual cortex in the back part of the brain?

Often, when we look at something we focus too hard, work at it too strenuously, creating tension and disrupting the flow of energy.

Have you ever thought about deep seeing? (It's like deep listening.)

Can we become quiet enough in our seeing to flow with the rhythms of life? To invite, inquire, and receive the flow of life?

❖ ❖ ❖ ❖ ❖ ❖ ❖

True 20/20 vision can only occur if we are open to an ever-expanding vision of our lives. Vision is more than seeing clearly in the physical world; we also have to keep our inner worlds in sight. Our eyes are connected with the deeper parts of our autonomic nervous systems, our endocrine systems, our immune systems, and our fluid bodies.

Did you know we are comprised of 90% water as prenatal beings and 70% water as adults?

Did you know the eyes and brain together make up 2% of our body weight and use 25% of our food intake?

90% of vision occurs in the mind, so the more our minds are filled with chatter, the busier our eyes will be and the worse we will see.

Factors outside our eyes can affect the eye tissue profoundly. If we eat a lot of junk food or have been exposed to heavy metal toxicities, our livers have to work extra hard. And remember, in Chinese medicine the liver is said to rule the eyes. Conditions like floaters and macular degeneration have their roots in liver chi stagnation.

80% of body tension is carried in the eyes. Our eyes are our major navigational system, and we often unconsciously store tension in our eyes, especially if a perceived threat triggers a flight or fight survival response.

Most of us have forgotten that it's possible to feel sensation in our eye tissues. If we don't know that our eyes are connected to many of our body systems (like our cranial sacral rhythm, our acupuncture meridians), and we believe our eyes are an isolated system, then in time this vital area becomes stiffer and more rigid, even numb, reducing the information flow to our eyes and brain.

But when we learn to slow down, everything changes. As we begin to relax our survival responses, the decrease in tension allows more nourishment to flow through the optic pathways to the brain. The eyes are made up mostly of fluid. This fluid carries memory and information, so as the flow becomes freer, we might become more aware of our eye tissue and of the ancient memories stored there.

❖ ❖ ❖ ❖ ❖ ❖ ❖

Filters can be very limiting, especially when we don't even realize we have them. Seeing *through* our eyes helps us to become aware of the unconscious filters we have placed in front of them. Whether the filters are cultural or tribal in origin, or even if we created them as an adaptive response to stress, once we become aware of them we can choose which to keep and which to let go.

❖ ❖ ❖ ❖ ❖ ❖ ❖

It's only because of light that our eyes can see. When light finds our eyes and our retinas' photo receptors are stimulated, our eyes move toward the light — and we begin to move in our journey through life. About 25 % of the light that enters the eyes travels to the hypothalamus, the part of the brain that directs our endocrine function. When light is broken down into its individual colors, the hypothalamus sends different frequencies to different parts of the body, helping to stimulate balance. The better we absorb the gift of light, the better we can radiate it, expressing our spirit as well as our vitality and creativity.

❖ ❖ ❖ ❖ ❖ ❖ ❖

As we begin to reflect and see inside ourselves, we can start to understand our nearsighted, farsighted, and astigmatism patterns. Remember, it is the programming the brain sends to our eyes that causes them to deteriorate.

Prescription lenses serve to validate this internal programming. The refractive measurement from which the lenses are made describes the scroll of history and story of a person's adaptive response to life. Each prescription represents a strategy we use to avoid seeing what life is showing us. We think that with our prescription we see more clearly, but really, it removes us further from truly seeing. The lens provides an artificial way of seeing through a prescribed filter. The person who thinks this is how we should see is not taking into account what our eyes are really expressing.

Can we find a better way of prescribing lenses? Some of us might want to try a "homeopathic" lens. Rather than forcing a vision correction externally, this solution provides a very tiny power of correction, allowing balance to come about from an internal place.

❖ ❖ ❖ ❖ ❖ ❖ ❖ ❖

Can we balance the clarity and blur? Maybe including a little blur in our visual experience would relax our visual system and bring us closer to balance. Too much clarity creates a stress response and can make it harder, not easier, to increase the energy flow into the eyes.

A little blur is about receiving life in a more vulnerable way, being in the right brain instead of the left brain, softening so that we can be more attuned to the subtle energies within ourselves and within life itself.

Blur helps us release the patterned addictions in our thinking, moving, and seeing. (It's hard to avoid falling into these responses in a society that seems to say we need to become more like machines.) Blur is about returning to our biological process of movement and flow. Blur reminds us about our deep capacity for trust. Blur, if we can relax into it, will help us see ourselves in a new way, and the by-product is more clarity, a clarity that we master from an internal place of peace and harmony, instead of from an external crutch like a lens. Blur says let go! Be, rather than do! Let's soften our survival response, be in the love instead of the fear.

The second eye-opener is: The way you heal your eyes is by embracing and loving your blur. Going into your blur gives you the gift of clarity, both from an internal place and in our physical world.

❖ ❖ ❖ ❖ ❖ ❖ ❖ ❖

Ilya Priogine, winner of the Nobel Peace Prize for his work on thermodynamics of nonequilibrium systems, states that the farther away we move from an equilibrium state (current habitual patterning—my meaning), the more we become aware of our external environment, and the more potential our system has to reorganize itself in very unusual and innovative ways. The system does so in a non-linear fashion.

Being in the blur jars us out of the state of equilibrium, and the possibilities abound. I have also experienced and observed this level of transformation when applying Continuum Movement, watching people inhabit their bodies through their fluid system in a whole new way!

In terms of our eyes, we have been entrained to believe that there is one way we are "supposed" to see. Eye doctors who have succumbed to mainstream allopathic indoctrination are afraid of blur — let's get rid of it right away! — so they prescribe a strong lens to hide the blur from you.

Myopia says our focus is too tight, thus the need to look through a minus or negative lens which creates more negativity and judgment in ourselves. Hyperopia and presbyopia says our focus is too diffused or flaccid, thus the need to look through a lens that creates artificial magnification, and astigmatism which says our focus is twisted, thus the need to look through a lens which creates a distorted view.

Yes, we need focus, but maybe we can organize and focus with relaxation and effortlessness. Are you seeking an emergence state or an emergency state? Let's find a way to focus while being inclusive, instead of focusing tightly and becoming exclusive and isolated.

Blur slows us down so we can be vulnerable, sense our bodies, and begin to recover from over-stimulation. We can return to Primitive Primordial Vision, where our eyes along with the skin, are an outgrowth of brain tissue and become our embryonic roots. We return to float in the womb. Our vestibular and peripheral vision begin to develop. Our eyes have to differentiate into many different cells: the retina (our light capturing system), the lens (helping us with focus), and our cornea (looking through the transparent window).

In blur, we can explore further. What is the state of our umbilical connection to mom? To the larger cosmos? What are the early imprints we receive from our parents' consciousness at preconception and conception? From our gestating experience? Remember that everything outside our bodies in-utero becomes our energy field...

In blur, we can invoke a trans-rational seeing, intuitive, non-linear, and subtle. Moving not only with our eyes but our bodies, we can become nourished, supported, replenished, and sustained.

CHAPTER THREE

THE MARRIAGE OF MATTER AND SPIRIT

As a child, I first awakened to energy by playing with magnetism. I was fascinated when I saw that I could rearrange iron filings on a piece of paper by moving a magnet beneath the paper. Intrigued by magnets' invisible power, I puzzled over the mystery of how they worked. When I was older and learned more about magnetism, I was still intrigued, hooked on this force that could organize matter and energy. In high school, as I began connecting what I learned about physics and chemistry with my love for astronomy, I started to wonder if life involved another level beyond the physical. And how did light fit into the equation? I would have to wait to explore that idea much later in my education.

In college, my biology classes and the research I observed focused exclusively on the molecular model. (Later, I learned that this research paradigm linked molecular science to the corporate world.) I asked myself, "Are we just a bag of molecules? Could there be something else in our body's make-up?" But when I raised these question in the biology department, only one professor answered – and he told me to go study philosophy. I did take a philosophy course, but I did not find the answers to my questions.

While in optometry school, I couldn't help noticing that most academic science was focused in whichever areas had the most corporate funding available. Even in vision science, all of the research was in the molecular world. At the same time, when I read physics research, I observed that almost every scientist rejected any inquiries about "the field" out of hand. Such ideas, they said, reeked of mysticism, had religious overtones, were out of place in scientific discussions.

For my whole life, long before I had a name for it, I was looking for answers about the energy that is in our bodies and all around us, which I have learned since to call "energy fields." An energy field is the energy that lies within and around the bodies of humans and other living beings. Our bodies emit a lot of energy. An infrared filter would reveal our bodies to be radiating at about 100 watts. That's a pretty bright light bulb!

The energy field hypothesis says the dynamical field conveys information and integration throughout the body. It is central to our integration, the primary regulator of our physiology and biochemistry, and supersedes molecular reactions. Our level of coherence is determined by mind, intent, awareness, and our higher self.

Throughout my professional life I have been fascinated by how light flows into our bodies and how it influences our health. Light is information flow, traveling in the form of waves, particles, or pulsation, mirroring the energy of the fluids in our bodies.

In optometry school, along with geometric and physiological optics, I was also learning about the movement of energy into our eyes. It occurred to me that the flow of energy out of the eyes must be just as important. Our eyes' inhalation and exhalation of light is one of the ways we create and change our reality. Another way to say this is that with our eyes we converge that which is flexion and diverge that which is extension. Most people are not able to exhale very well with their vision.

❖ ❖ ❖ ❖ ❖ ❖ ❖

I began my first practice outside Philadelphia in the mid-'80s and around the same time joined a group called The College of Syntonic Optometry. In the practice of Syntonics, optometrists use colored lenses, gels, and lights to apply light and color through the eyes and into the body. The College was started in 1934 by medical doctor and optometrist Harry Riley Spitler. When Dr. Spitler applied different color frequencies to the eyes of mental patients, he had such resounding success that he developed an entire protocol for treating emotional problems in this way. When I began using some of Spitler's light therapy protocols with my patients and measured the results, I

I SENSE: AT PLAY IN THE FIELD OF HEALING

found that this treatment improved peripheral vision, with resulting improvement of both overall eyesight and body balance.

By observing patients' visual patterns, I learned that adaptive responses to stress, trauma, or toxicity can cause the retina to become desensitized to light and create suppression, or a blind spot, in the visual field. Visual suppression is usually a functional shut-down due to stress, as though the person is saying "I am overwhelmed and don't want to see what is right in front of me."

Unfortunately, most eye doctors give relatively limited examinations and, except in cases of glaucoma, stroke incidents, or macular degeneration, usually miss suppression in their assessments. Since they only recognize suppression in patients who have those particular conditions, they may diagnose any cases of suppression as being due to one of them, even if the cause is something very different. Because of this, many patients have ended up with further eye damage and scarring due to use of unneeded and inappropriate surgical procedures and medications.

Light therapy quickly became a keystone of my practice. Working with patients with visual suppression, I developed protocols using different lights and colors, stimulating and re-sensitizing the photoreceptor cells on the retina. I found that this practice helped children improve their visual fields – which helped them to balance better, have better memories, and become more adept in both sports and schoolwork. I also treated elderly patients with macular degeneration and glaucoma and had great success using light therapy to reverse eye disease.

I now understood that by modifying the way light enters a person's eyes, we can change that person's life. Changing the light distribution onto the retina with its 137 million photo receptors, treats the whole patient, respecting the integrity of our bodies and our health. Homeopathic lenses work in a similar way. They are a very small plus prescription that have nothing to do with improving the optics of the eyes and everything to do with increasing the light energy into the eyes. They work by spreading the light in a more equal fashion into the eyes. By increasing the energy into the eyes, people experience more peripheral vision and a deeper eye-body relaxation.

✦ ✦ ✦ ✦ ✦ ✦ ✦

In 1994, while writing my first book, I met Dr. Hazel Parcells, a woman who changed my life. She was 103 years old at that time and just opening a new retreat center in Sapello, New Mexico. A naturopath and chiropractor, she had developed a variety of methods for healing the body using subtle energy therapies and health-based foods.

Dr. Parcells agreed to meet with me at her Center, and as soon as we met, I knew that I wanted to spend as much time as possible studying with her. Her methods focused on observing and working with the body's subtle energy in ways that I found new, exciting, and at times almost unbelievable.

She questioned each person's body and energy on physical, emotional, and spiritual levels. One technique she used was scanning the body's energy patterns using a dowsing method with a pendulum.

Another method was to take a small sample of a client's blood – she called it a "blood spot" – and ask a variety of questions while using a specially designed board with a pendulum. The pendulum's movements allowed her to measure the vibratory rates of the person's blood, glands, and organs, endocrine, digestive, musculoskeletal, and reproductive systems, and also things like acid-alkaline balance, cholesterol, toxicities, psychological-emotional traumas, and chakras. Once Dr. Parcells had the measurements she needed, she performed a restorative process by broadcasting subtle energy frequencies, including homeopathy, color, sound, gems, and crystals, that she determined would help to bring the body back into balance.

Astonishingly to me, most of Dr. Parcells' clients lived in other geographical locations. Some lived halfway around the world! Dr. Parcells introduced me to the idea that our energy fields are not tied to our locations. She could use that small blood spot, which she called a witness of the person, to represent a person's energy pattern. It gave her the information she needed and, amazingly to me, received the treatment she provided. Thanks to her use of this witness, people could receive her healings without being physically present.

This concept blew my mind. While I'd never accepted my optometry training's message that most eye problems can only be treated with lenses, surgery, and pharmaceuticals, my left brain had a very hard time with the idea that there is such a thing as a non-local energy field – that individuals' energy fields can be changed at a distance. But I observed that most of Dr. Parcells' clients were getting well, even those with very serious health problems, and I begin to accept her theories. I could not necessarily see or understand the energies she was providing to people, but her results healing cancer and other serious maladies showed me that her treatments were indeed able to help others from a distance.

I observed that people who received these energies often found themselves confronting deeply held belief systems and attitudes that kept them fixed in negative patterns. As they chose to transform these long-held beliefs and accept responsibility for their own well-being, they not only started to heal from their diseases, but their external circumstances usually changed as well. That is, their internal climates reflected their external lives. As they raised their energetic vibration, they regained their physical wellness. When asked, these individuals tended to use words like "vibrant" and "joyful" to describe their lives.

I loved my opportunities to talk with Dr. Parcells. She was full of wisdom. Here are a few of the gems I collected from our conversations:

— The potential for illness can be seen in the energy field before it manifests in physical problems.
— Lower frequency disease patterns like cancer, MS, and fibromyalgia can't survive in a higher vibrational environment. So if we clean up our inner environments, those maladies should start to fade away.
— We each have to take full responsibility for our own health. Dis-ease is the body's way of saying that something is out of balance, and the longer we ignore the signals, the more the condition will manifest.
— Physical discomfort usually occurs in proportion to our resistance to change. If we choose health, we are choosing to live in a more authentic way. We must address the underlying

causes of our problems before we can receive the payoffs of vibrant health.

I studied and worked with Dr. Parcells for 2½ years. Finally, at the age of 106, she decided to transition to another state of consciousness and leave the physical plane.

❖ ❖ ❖ ❖ ❖ ❖ ❖

Over the years, I observed the amazing improvement that treatments like light and color therapy bring to patients' vision and to other aspects of their lives as well. Dr. Parcells stimulated my thinking further, forcing me to recognize that our energy fields lie not only within the body, but also surround it and are connected to a more global non-local field. Being part scientist, I began looking for a way to measure the energy changes in the body. I wanted to be able to quantitatively measure energy, but that aspect would have to wait. As it happened, it would be almost fifteen years until it was time for that project to manifest.

❖ ❖ ❖ ❖ ❖ ❖ ❖

Energy fields have been recognized and discussed in many ways in different times and places. In Eastern thought and healing practices, concepts like prana and chi speak of universal light energy fields.

Energy fields have also been discussed in western studies of embryology. In the recent past, Rupert Sheldrake has proposed that a *morphogenetic field* is the driving force of development, having more influence than genes or chromosomes. He has written a great deal on the power of our morphogenetic resonance with our ancestors, describing why certain family patterns are passed down through the energetic field and not just through DNA. This meshes with discoveries in epigenetics, where scientists are saying that genes are not static, but can be turned on and off by environmental factors.

Biofield science is an exciting part of Frontier Medicine developed by biophysicist Dr. Beverly Rubik. Dr. Rubik coined the expression "biofield" to refer to the energy field that lies within and around the body, sometimes described as an active, organizing field of life. *Kirlian photography* reveals the energy fields around objects, and studying Kirlian photos of the human body, I recognized that all structures in our bodies act as antennas. We emit energies from within the body and receive energies from our environment and from the stream of light energy, or *biophotons*, within.

❖ ❖ ❖ ❖ ❖ ❖ ❖

As I began to explore energy fields, I became increasingly aware of the rift between science and spirituality, and at the same time I began realizing we truly are more than just molecules. Mainstream western science says we are local, finite, material beings, period. But the new science that is emerging says that we are more than just physical bodies and that energy fields are simultaneously local and non-local. These new scientists describe energy fields that are rich in information. One example is Dr. Bruce Lipton's research in the area of epigenetics. Dr. Lipton, a cell biologist, has expanded the field of genetics, saying that DNA is turned on and off by environmental influences. It is the energy that creates the change....

Since I started studying energy fields, I've discovered that many scientists are actively researching and writing about this topic. Biophysicists like Beverly Rubik and quantum physicists like Claude Swanson found that every biological structure receives energy both from the environment and from within the body, and emits energy to the environment.

More and more, the new energy sciences are proving that the fields around us are dynamic, that they convey information, and that the biofield helps regulate the body's biochemistry and physiology. We have learned ways to measure an individual's biofield, revealing where the field shows compressions, traumas, toxicities, the influence of electronics, and other influences. In my practice, I have observed that the energy field changes almost immediately when I apply light therapy.

— The biofield is a bridge between the physical and metaphysical bodies.

— The biofield is a symphony, conducted by the mind, intent, awareness, and higher self.
— The biofield is a standing wave.
— The biofield influences our level of coherence – how well the energy waves or particles are aligned and in rhythm with each other.
— The more coherent our biofield, the more we are able to connect to the biolink, our bio-intelligence for healing.

❖ ❖ ❖ ❖ ❖ ❖ ❖

I learned that there are several ways to measure the biofield. Conventional medicine uses the EKG waves of the heart and the EEG waves of the brain. Other techniques include thermography, electrodermal measurements, and Kirlian photography. I was drawn to Kirlian photography, developed in the 1940s when Seymour Kirlian, an electrician, began observing auras by running a low voltage electric current through different living things and measuring the patterns created by the discharge of energy.

❖ ❖ ❖ ❖ ❖ ❖ ❖

For my work, I settled on the Gas Discharge Visualization (GDV) camera, a biomedical instrument invented by Russian biophysicist Konstantin Korotkov. The GDV camera is a scientific instrument whose results are quantifiable and consistent, creating digital-like Kirlian photography. This fascinating device bridges our understanding of the unseen world of energy with our knowledge of the physical world, capturing images of the living energy fields around people, other animals, plants, water, and more. It can measure the transfer and levels of photons within the body, including the energy levels in the meridians and chakras.

With this tool, it's possible to measure the biofields of living beings, food, water, essential oils, light, sound, crystals... and more. Almost every part of the human body, including our tissues, fascia, bone marrow, lymph system, cerebral spinal fluid, and blood, is composed mostly of fluid, and is therefore an excellent transmitter of energy. Our energies tend to be repeatable and stable and at the same time are influenced by the many cycles of our lives, including moon cycles, day-night cycles, seasonal cycles, and more. It is possible to measure the increase in the body's energy when we add subtle energies like light, sound, or essential oils to living things. We can also measure the decrease in energy when we add synthetic products, like pharmaceuticals.

If I wanted to use my GDV camera to get an image of your energetic levels, I would ask you to place your fingertips, one at a time, on a highly charged glass plate. You might feel a slight tickle each time you place a finger on the camera lens. (We use the fingertips because they are the endpoints of the major acupuncture meridians, and the information we receive from this area correlates closely with health and disease.) The electrical charge induces a discharge of energy from each finger, which the camera captures. Its software then produces a sequence of light patterns representing the energy discharges. Through mathematical analysis and optics, it extracts the data from these patterns and plots the energy associated with the various organs, tissues, and glands on each side of your body.

A lot of qualitative thinking goes into interpreting these patterns, and once I have reviewed the data, I have access to a wealth of information about your past and present, including traumas, acute and chronic health problems from physical, emotional, psychological, and spiritual perspective, and the size and alignment of your chakras. With this information, I am better able to suggest next steps for your treatment on an energetic level.

If we measure the same person three days in a row, always at the same time and taking into account the person's circadian rhythms, we will see identical energy patterns each time. These patterns are referred to as a person's energetic signature.

Extensive studies conducted starting in 1997 have shown that the GDV's results are repeatable, reproducible, and quantifiable, and it is increasingly used alongside more conventional diagnostic techniques. Its use has been accepted by Russian Academy of Science, and practitioners in this country are hopeful that it will soon be accepted here as well.

I have found that the numerical data produced by GDV science is a powerful tool, offering insight into our health on the biological level as well as the state our ecosystems on an energetic level.

Another of Dr. Korotkov's devices, the Eco Sensor, measures light activity to give us information about the energy in spaces, structures, and the environment. Its data can help us to understand the emotions, intention, and focus of people in those spaces. Dr. Korotkov has used the Eco Sensor to research the energy of temples and other sacred spaces around the world. In my own experience with it, I have seen how our thoughts create and affect our reality. Our environment is changed by the energy we emit into the field.

❖ ❖ ❖ ❖ ❖ ❖ ❖

I have been exploring many hypotheses in my own research with energy and healing.
— All living things are interrelated and interconnected.
— All living things communicate through both biological and electromagnetic fields.
— All living things can affect and be affected by both planetary energetic fields and the Earth's magnetic fields.
— Both magnetic and bio-energetic fields affect our body rhythms, which include our heart rate, breathing pattern, fluid resonance, nervous system, and brain waves.
— If all living things broadcast love, compassion, and gratitude, we could offset the current incoherence and stress waves that surround us.

Chronobiology

This field of biology explores Earth, solar, and lunar rhythms as they relate to our own biology. Our bodies have energetic sensitivity to many of these forces.

Geomagnetic fields emanate from the Earth's core as invisible lines. Without them life on earth would not be possible: they create a static field that extends above the Earth's atmosphere, shielding us from solar flares and solar winds. These invisible lines flex like guitar strings, influencing our body rhythms, affecting our brains, nervous systems, memory and concentration, endocrine function, heart coherence, and fluid bodies.

Magnetic fields in our atmosphere also affect and influence us. One, in the ionosphere, is an energy field with the form of a soft plasma bubble. Its strong magnetic field influences our bodies. The Schumann Resonance, located between the Earth and the ionosphere, is another magnetic wave form that affects us. It vibrates at a frequency of 7.8 Hz, which is concurrent with our brains' alpha waves when experiencing a state of well-being and harmony within ourselves.

The moon's energy also affects our body rhythms, especially during the full lunar cycle.

Many ancient cultures wrote about how solar activity affects all living things, and scientists are now reporting that solar flares affect human body rhythms.

They have recognized a correlation between solar flares, which can also be called energetic influxes, and increased human excitability. My question is, can we be in touch with our rhythms enough to flourish during these flares?

I believe we are being called to take responsibility for our own energy and to connect more deeply with Mother Earth's energy. If we listen to and feel these Earth waves, we can come together and connect. We can be in touch with our rhythms enough to flourish during solar flares. We can join forces with Mother Earth to use her energy in a positive, coherent way.

Each atom on our skin emits 2000 photons per second – all of this light goes out into the ethers like low level starlight – we know no limit. We are glowing and all the light we emit goes to the far reaches of the universe. We are sensitive antennas, sending out and receiving energy. Our energy fields are active organizing fields of life.

The third eye opener is that our energy both shapes and is shaped by our environment. When we collectively produce more love, harmony, and compassion, we are creating a world with less violence.

I SENSE: AT PLAY IN THE FIELD OF HEALING

CHAPTER FOUR

NATURE'S APOTHECARY

The fourth eye opener is that embracing our limitations frees us to become limitless.

Pure medicinal essential oils offer amazingly versatile gifts for healing. Working with these essences, I am often able to address my patients' vision and health problems and help them with deeper issues as well. Because of the complexity of these essences, they are useful for a great many conditions, offering healing in the physical, emotional, and spiritual realms.

Medicinal essences can be applied to help reduce symptoms, and they can also be used in ritual or ceremony, or to anoint each other as an act of love. I have used them to work with specific physical and emotional problems, to soften the survival response and subconscious belief systems, and to help people reconnect with Earth Mother. Used correctly, essential oils are powerful healers on all levels.

In this chapter, I will share information about using pure medicinal essential oils for healing on the physical level. These essences also bring many spiritual gifts, and we will talk more about that in Chapter 7.

"Grace", age seventy two was diagnosed with a cataract in her right eye. She came to see me for a second opinion and some possible treatment options. I recommended she use five essences around the eyes: Saffron, Laurel Leaf, Clary Sage, Carrot Seed, and Frankincense, three times a day for a month. After one month, she returned and her cataract had reduced by 50%. I had her continue the treatment for three months and at the end of the three months, her cataract had completely gone away. When the essences are used around the eyes, they bring a great deal of oxygenation and at the same time dissolve free radical accumulation in the eye tissues (a main cause of cataract formation).

❖ ❖ ❖ ❖ ❖ ❖ ❖

"Jan", age forty two, attended one of my Medicinal Essential Oils Certification classes. When she called me a few months later, she had been diagnosed with fibroids and was frustrated that her current doctor felt surgery was required to remove them. Jan and her husband were trying to get pregnant and wanted to avoid surgery if possible, and she knew that I had helped other women with similar conditions by using an essential oils protocol.

My fibroid protocol uses twelve different essences. I instructed Jan to apply these essences to a tampon each day and insert the tampon, removing it after six hours. She was to repeat a second time before bed, removing the tampon in the morning. I asked her to follow this protocol for 30 days or until her next menstrual cycle. I also recommended that during this time, she should be sure to process any emotional or spiritual issues that came up around the second chakra, which relates to the sexual organs and sexuality. Jan diligently followed this protocol. After the first month, her ultrasound showed a 30% size reduction. Since she was making progress, I suggested she use this protocol for two more months, and when she went back for another ultrasound, the fibroids were completely gone.

❖ ❖ ❖ ❖ ❖ ❖ ❖

The above treatment is not widely accepted by mainstream, popular aromatherapists. I want to be clear that there is a big difference between the popular conception and practice of aromatherapy and the use of high quality essential oils for medicinal aromatherapy. Jan's example showed how effective essences can be for shrinking tumors and growths of all kinds. They have many other amazing aspects too, and when we deeply connect to the medicine they offer, we can bring our bodies back to balance.

Aromatherapy has been exploited by the corporate world and has now reached fad status, with adulterated or pre-mixed blends of essential oils for sale at every natural food store and new age shop. They may smell nice, but there is very little healing value in these mass produced oils that have been adulterated or diluted and processed into soaps, perfumes, and other products. And as for pre-mixed blends, it is much more effective to use single essences and layer with others when needed. The single essences have a much higher vibration than pre-mixed blends.

I can't emphasize strongly enough how important it is to use pure raw medicinal grade therapeutic essential oils, whether you are seeking healing or spiritual growth. Unfortunately, the less complex an essential oil, the easier it is to adulterate. And the more expensive or scarce an essential oil, the higher the seduction for adulteration. The main consumers of adulterated oils are perfumers, producers of aromatics, and the soap industry. The international flavor market also accepts adulteration because it is solely profit-oriented. As long as oils for aromatherapy represent a tiny fraction of the world production of essential oils, the danger of bad quality oils in aromatherapy will continue.

Always be sure you know that the essences you are working with are of high quality. The source of your essences is very important in medicinal applications. Each essence contains different active chemical ingredients, known as chemotypes, each of which has a specific influence on the plant. The complexity of the essences allows them to work with a variety of different conditions and represents Nature's intelligence on a very subtle level.

I purchase my essential oils from a company called Wisdom of the Earth. These are the purest raw essences I can find, with nothing added or removed, so they have the highest vibration possible for healing and for physical and spiritual growth. Using Wisdom of the Earth's essences to help people with cancer, Parkinson's disease, and other health problems, I have seen that they offer healing at physical, emotional, and spiritual levels.

How to apply medical essential oils

Therapeutic grade essential oils can be applied topically, taken sublingually and orally, or even applied vaginally or rectally. Please be gentle when first starting to use medicinal essences. I like to start by breathing in their aroma and then take as much time as necessary to feel what my body does with the energy. The more we slow down, the more we can connect to our own rhythms, and this practice helps us nourish and reconnect to our depleted selves.

In my work, I have found that medicinal essences work most powerfully when single essences are applied or layered on the body. Each essence represents an incredibly complex blend created by Mother Nature, and my experience is that pre-mixing essential oils negatively affects their vibrational energy and healing power.

TOPICAL USE: In my private sessions and workshops, I teach the application of the essences "neat" – that is, directly on the skin, undiluted. While some practitioners may say that essences must always be blended in a carrier oil and should never be put directly on the skin, I have found that the greatest medicinal power is achieved by using the essences undiluted.

When using essences on the skin, sometimes it can be important to apply or layer them in a certain order. Oils which have a Yang, or hot, quality, like Oreganos or Clove Bud, tend to be skin irritants and should be used with great care on the skin. Using a "cold-hot-cold" format allows you to safely apply such essences almost anywhere on the body. I recommend beginning and ending with an essence that has a Yin, or cool quality. Apply the sensitive or hot essence(s) in between, using slightly fewer drops to assure that the area they cover is within the "boundaries" of the area covered by the initial Yin essence.

I highly recommend keeping essences away from the mouth, eyes, and mucous membranes. But do not be alarmed if a few drops do get in one of these sensitive areas; while it will be quite uncomfortable for 15-30 minutes, it will not do permanent damage. To alleviate the discomfort, you can apply a pure oil like olive oil or coconut oil to the area to neutralize the irritating effect of the essence. For the eye area, dab a few drops around the outside of the eye...*never put the neutralizing oil in the eye.*

While for the most part essences do not have side effects, they may cause skin irritation, either because of a reaction to the essence itself or because the essence triggers a detoxification reaction (which is a good thing!). ALWAYS DO A TEST PATCH when using a new essence, and consider skin type (fair skinned? more sensitive than most?) when selecting and applying essences. Tip for those with sensitive skin: the soles of the feet are full of receptors and can usually take any essence.

However careful we are, almost everyone will have a skin reaction one time or another when using the essences. This is because the skin is a major dumping ground for hidden toxicities that are stored in the tissues, and the essences are great detoxifiers. If the skin reaction is extreme, either use some essences to help neutralize the skin reaction or reduce the dosage until the skin reaction clears.

The most powerful (i.e.medically effective) way to apply medicinal essences is topically...directly on the skin, undiluted (neat). The average absorption rate is 50%.

The first rule of aromatherapy is to apply the essence(s) on the area of concern, or as close as possible to it (e.g., for a headache at the temples, apply the essence(s) to the temple area; for an eye, apply around the outside of the eye socket). Literally ANY essence can be applied "neat" to the soles of the feet, regardless of its temperature or skin sensitivity. When using more than one essence, they should be layered, one at a time, on the skin. Massage each gently into the skin before applying the next essence.

AURICULAR USE: Application behind the ears is great for head congestion, headaches, sinus problems, general malaise, and cold and flu symptoms. This is a very powerful treatment option! Use about five drops each of 5-7 essences. Apply them on the area about midway behind the ear down to the bottom of the neck, layering over the eustachian tubes. Put the first essence behind one ear, then the other ear, and continue going back and forth until you have used all your selected essences. Use respiratory essences, antihistamine essences, antibacterial essences.

ORAL USE of essences should be approached with care and only done under the supervision of an experienced aromatherapist. The digestive process breaks down the essences, so oral usage is generally not as powerful as topical, but this method can be used in conjunction with topical application for an additive effect. The average absorption rate with oral usage is 20-25%.

SUBLINGUALLY (under the tongue) is more effective than swallowing the essence due to the higher level of receptors in this area. The average absorption rate there is 30-35%.

VAGINAL AND RECTAL USE: Application of the essences vaginally (through a douche or tampon) or rectally yields an average absorption rate of 50% +. While it is often reported that absorption in these areas is comparable to the outer skin, they may offer slightly greater absorption due to the lack of an external evaporative factor.

Usually, vaginal application is done via an organic cotton tampon (10-12 drops of relevant essences dripped on to the tip of the tampon, then inserted) or a travel douche (about 20 drops in tepid water, depending upon the situation). Tampon application is more powerful; also it is possible to "layer" skin sensitive essences this way. Rectal application is usually done via suppository. Score an organic, glycerin suppository with a sharp knife, drip the essence(s) into the opening, then gently close it back up and insert into rectum), or via a Fleet disposable enema (about 20 drops, depending upon the situation). You can also place several drops on the tip of your finger and place it gently inside the opening of the rectum.

INHALATION is a great application for sinus problems, respiratory congestion, lung infections, etc. Boil a cup or mug of water (preferably on the stove, not in a microwave), then add your essences. Some essences that are commonly used in this approach are the Eucalyptuses, Pines, Spruces, Peppermints, Laurel Leaf, Himalayan Soti, and Tea Tree. If you are using three or four essences, put about 5-7 drops of each in the hot water and hold a towel over your head, making a tent over the cup, capturing the steam... breath deeply, inhaling the essences carried by the steam. When the water cools, drink it. I have seen that people who use this protocol for bacterial infections may completely avoid the need for antibiotics.

HOW MUCH TO USE: Determining how many drops of essence to use is an art, not a science. "One size does not fit all." Every situation is different and must be considered individually. Also, the application method influences how much of the essence will be absorbed by the body. Here are some factors to consider.

How serious is the condition? For someone in a crisis situation you might use more than for "routine maintenance."

A person's height and weight are important. The larger the person, the more drops one uses. A good place to start is 8-10 drops each of up to four or five essences if the person is of average height and weight. For a large or overweight person, the amount should be increased accordingly. For a small or underweight person, the amount should be decreased.

Other factors make a difference too. Consider the person's eating habits, exercise level, and emotional state. People with unhealthy lifestyles need larger amounts of the essences than people with unhealthy lifestyles. Age makes a difference. For elders, children, and infants, the amount used should be reduced. Since working with babies and children requires much judgment and discretion, it is best to consult an experienced medicinal aromatherapist until you have developed depth in this area. Pregnancy makes a difference too. Once again, it is best to consult an experienced medicinal aromatherapist until you have developed depth in this area.

What about pharmaceuticals?

Medicinal essences do not work as well for users who are taking pharmaceutical medications. Pharmaceuticals, which are synthetic, make us more susceptible to disease. A person who uses pharmaceuticals and wants to try essences should consider whether they want to use both modes of treatment, or whether they want to work with their health provider to wean themselves off the meds before starting treatment with essences.

I strongly advocate using medicinal essential oils instead of pharmaceutical drugs whenever possible, for many reasons. First, unlike pharmaceuticals, essential oils almost never cause side effects. Second, while drug resistance is a big problem with "single action" pharmaceuticals, microorganisms don't develop resistance to essential oils because of their incredible complexity (each essence is made up of 50,000-65,000 chemotypes). Furthermore, pharmaceutical antibiotics kill all microorganisms they come in contact with, both good and bad, because they cannot distinguish between them. But essences can recognize the beneficial bugs and only kill those that do harm. Finally, single action pharmaceutical drugs do what they are "programmed" to do: lower blood pressure, kill bacteria, increase thyroid production. They are not designed to increase over-all well-being. But medicinal essences bring the body's systems into balance. Essences that work with blood pressure, bring it into balance; essences that work with thyroid functioning, bring it into balance; essences that are anti-bacterial only kill the harmful bacteria... bringing the body back into balance, all while supporting the immune system.

Frequency Research

The megahertz frequencies of medicinal essences can be measured using a frequency counter or oscilloscope, which counts the number of occurrences of a repeating current flow per second. The higher the frequency the greater the amount of potency for healing and well-being.

Frequencies of the human body
    Healthy body (62-68 MHz)
    Disease begins, colds invade (59-60 MHz)
    Flu-like symptoms (58 MHz)
    Viral Infection (55 MHz)
    Epstein Barr (52 MHz)
    Tissue breakdown from disease (48 MHz)
    Cancer (42 MHz)

Frequencies of some essential essences (these vary by batch, soil, weather conditions, etc.)
Rose (320 MHz)
Helichrysum (181 MHz)
Tansy, Wild (105 MHz)
Lavender (118 MHz)
Melissa (102 MHz)

Here are a few remedies that I recommend for specific physical and emotional problems.

BASIL (EXOTICA, SWEET): Reduces muscle spasms and headaches, helps reduce digestive problems.

BLACK CUMIN: Great immune builder, high in vitamins, minerals and protein. Helps reduce skin disease.

CHAMOMILES (BLUE, ROMAN, WILD): Increases emotional relaxation and helpful for insomnia. Also can be used for reducing skin dermatitis. I use Wild Chamomile for softening our survival circuits.

EUCALYPTUS: Another good immune stimulant. Works well as an anti-bacterial and expectorant. I also use it to increase mental clarity.

ELEMI, MYRRH, and GALBANUM: These help the glandular, respiratory, and immune systems.

FIR and FIR NEEDLE: Great for adrenal support, very grounding, effective analgesic, and also anti-bacterial.

GERANIUM: Helps to balance hormones, especially in menopause. Also useful in helping us adjust to new life transitions.

GOLDENROD: Kidney and bladder tonic and offers anti-inflammatory properties. Excellent heart tonic on all levels.

LAVENDER ALBANIAN WILD HARVEST: Great for burns, headaches, and relaxing the heart and opening to self-love. Also very calming.

MUGWORT: A great anti-fungal and anti-parasite formula. Helps reduce anxiety. I use it to move out blocked or stuck energy on the physical, emotional, and spiritual levels.

NIAOULI (MQV): Excellent for protecting us from radiation (along with Spike Lavender) and great for treating food poisoning. Very uplifting.

PEPPERMINT: Useful for nervous, hepatic, skin, circulatory, immune, intestinal, and psychological disorders.

SPIKENARD: Very relaxing, used for insomnia. Reduces the survival response.

VETIVER: Cooling and stress-reducing. Softens the edges while grounding.

ZANTHOXYLUM: Improves digestion and facilitates tooth and gum health. Great for reducing anxiety.

Wisdom of the Earth offers over 225 single essences. When I teach my two-day aromatherapy certification course, I introduce people to many of these essences.

The Eye Protocol

In my years of studying and treating eye problems, I have found that in most cases, a large part of the problem is that the eye tissue is starved for nutrients. Our eyes need a great deal of oxygenation, as well as high amounts of glutathione, vitamin C, beta carotene, B complex, and other vitamins and minerals. Many people with vision problems also suffer from toxicities. The liver is always involved when someone is dealing with toxicity, and we know from Chinese medicine that the liver rules the eyes. I have found that the medicinal essences offer many properties for both nourishment and detoxification.

Here are some of my "go to essences" for the eyes.

CARROT SEED improves the eyes by protecting against macular degeneration, detoxifying blood vessels, toning the liver, relieving stress and anxiety, and providing many nourishing vitamins and minerals.

FRANKINCENSE has been around since antiquity, a sacred plant that can be helpful in showing us our visual blind spots. Frankincense tells us to "open up that third eye" and is my main "go to" around the eyes.

SAFFRON is very helpful for eye health as it helps rebalance body fluids on a cellular level and stimulates the Chi in the entire body. It contains high levels of antioxidants, vitamins, and minerals.

SWEET FENNEL, with its spicy sweet scent similar to black licorice, is a detoxifier, blood purifier, and diuretic, reduces swelling, headaches, and dizziness, and restores and stimulates the overall digestive system.

To use the following protocols for some common eye problems, I recommend layering each essence below the eyes and about 2-3 inches above the eyes at the temples. Do this 2-3 times per day. If you get an essence in your eyes, dab a little coconut oil near the edge the eye to neutralize the burning (never in the eye). Don't use water or saline – they will cause the eyes to "burn more".

Night Vision/ Overall General Tonic
1. Sweet Fennel
2. Saffron
3. Carrot Seed
4. Frankincense

Dry Eye
1. Carrot Seed
2. Frankincense
3. Clary Sage (endocrine balance)

Glaucoma
1. Laurel Leaf (for lymph)
2. Saffron (this is also a yang essence and should be layered
3. Frankincense
4. Spike Lavender (great analgesic)

Cataracts
1. Laurel Leaf
2. Clary Sage
3. Saffron
4. Frankincense
5. Carrot Seed

Using Medicinal Essences To Work With Cancer:

FRANKINCENSE, GALBANUM, and **MYRRH** are the three strongest anti-cancer medicinal essences. These essences can cross through the blood-brain barrier to help improve the immune system and create more access to healing potency.

ROSE, NEROLI, and **HELICHRYSUM ITALICUM:** These blossom essences are high intensity and vibrate at a very high frequency, creating an inhospitable environment for cancer cells.

BLACK CUMIN and **TURMERIC:** Black Cumin is a great immune booster and Turmeric has the quality of shrinking tumors. Twice a day, add 10 drops to a cup of hot tea and drink it.

MEXICAN LIME and **TURMERIC:** Turmeric has the quality of shrinking tumors and Mexican Lime has a high anti-cancer quality as well. Apply these essential oils to the area of concern.

ONION and **GARLIC:** These medicinal essences also offer anti-cancer properties but be aware – the smell is intense!

Using Medicinal Essential Oils with Animals

Many people who have seen the many gifts of medicinal essences want to learn about using these natural healers with their domestic animals. Tresa Laferty is an animal communicator, aromatherapist, and reiki healer who has taught me a great deal about how to help animals. One of Tresa's main teachings is to respect the animals, and check in with them before applying any medicinal essence. *(See resource section to contact Tresa.)*

There are different ways to assess which essences to use with dogs and cats. Be sure to proceed slowly and mindfully, as their noses – especially dogs' – are way more sensitive than ours. Use these steps each time you introduce new essences to an animal.

— Give the animal a choice of two or three essences. Open the bottles slightly and place in different parts the room. That way the animal can move closer – or leave the room if it doesn't like them. Observe which the animal is most interested in.

— Hold a bottle near the animal's nose and observe the response. You can also put the essential oil on your hands, a tissue, or cotton ball. (Don't force it under the animal's nose – be respectful of the animal's space.)

As you do this, here are a few things to remember.
— Dogs often analyze each smell in a very detailed and intense way.
— Animals are most likely to be attracted to plants that they have smelled or eaten in nature.
— As you progress, you will come to understand the animal's "yes" and "no" signals.
— Even if they don't like an essence today, this does not mean they won't like it tomorrow and visa versa. Animals are very intuitive and always select what they need. The key is trusting them!
— Don't forget, animals know what they need better than what we do.

If the animal wants you to proceed, here are three ways to apply the essences.
— The best and easiest option is to use a diffuser to distribute the essence into the room.
— The second option is to apply topically to the skin, hair, or fur. Put a few drops on your hands and have a love fest! If they happen to lick the part of their body with the essence, this won't be a problem as long as you just use a little bit topically.
— The third option is to have the animal ingest the essence by adding a specific quantity to their food, but this must be started very slowly. I recommend getting guidance from an aromatherapist who has experience working with animals.

Here are a few general tips based on my own experiences using medicinal essences with animals.
— Many animals have excellent memories, so introduce the essences slowly and lovingly to make sure they have a positive first experience.
— Because of dogs' acute sense of smell, any essence will affect them much more quickly than it would us.
— Start with calming essences before you use essences for treatment.
— Animals tend to like Lemon, Basil, Rosemary.
— If we wear the essence ourselves, the animal associates it with us. Also, this unifies the field created by the medicinal essence, amplifying the animal's healing.

— If the animal's health condition is acute or serious, try to connect with the animal's higher self. Respect whatever response you receive.

Tips for using essences topically:
— I like to apply the oils to the fur or feathers, as these body parts act as wicks and pull the essence into the body. You can also apply them directly to the skin, proceeding slowly and observing any reaction the animal may have.
— An alternative is to put a drop on their bedding or a towel.
— If you are going to use multiple oils (layering), start with one oil and observe for 15 minutes. Then, if there is no negative reaction, add the second. Repeat for any additional essences.
— The pads of the feet are very sensitive. Many dogs and cats have an aversion to having their pads touched. I don't apply essences here unless they have an injury in this area.
— Other areas like the base of the spine, along the spine, the shoulders, chest, the tummy, and under the chin are all possibilities.
— Dosage: Medium and large size dogs 3-5 drops.
  Small dogs and cats 1-2 drops. Most cats, less than one drop.

Use extra caution in sensitive areas like the eyes and ears.
— The essences can be applied to the edges of the ears by putting the essence on your hand and rubbing it on the outside of the ear. Never use in the ear canal.
— For the eyes, I use a Hydrosol of Rose and Helichrysum. I dilute 50/50 with saline solution and do a "test" on my own eyes first. If it burns my eyes, the spray is too strong and needs to be diluted more.

Common Essences Used for Animals
FOR PAIN OR INFLAMMATION: Birch, Red Spruce, Frankincense, Wintergreen
FOR THUNDERSTORMS, ANXIETY, OR STRESS: Laurel Leaf, Orange Blood Red, Bergamot, Albanian Lavender
FOR HYPERACTIVE DOGS OR CALMING: Fir Balsam, Zanthoxylum, Lemon

FOR INCREASING CONFIDENCE OR INSTILLING COURAGE: Laurel Leaf, any of the Spruces, Orange Blood Red
FOR RESCUE ANIMALS: Geranium, Rosewood, Hyssop
FOR IMMUNE SUPPORT: Black Cumin, Frankincense, Clove
FOR FLEAS AND TICKS (both prevention and treatment of bites): Marjoram, Lemon Eucalpytus, Patchouli, Artemesia, Citronella
FOR SORE MUSCLES OR STIFF JOINTS: Birch, Black Spruce, Spike Lavender, Mugwort
FOR CLEANING CRATES, BOWLS, AND BUCKETS: Lemon, Rosemary, Camphor
FOR ANIMALS NEARING DEATH: Frankincense, Palo Santo, Hyssop, Laurel Leaf

A Choice for Healing and Growth

Therapeutic essences derived from plants offer a wonderful, powerful, and subtle choice for healing and growth. They match with the human organism in an intrinsic way and, like a key and lock, fill in the "energy holes" created by our ailments.

Anointing the essences on a loved one can be a sacred and divine process, a rite of passage that helps align and balance the integration of mind-body-spirit. Using the essences in ceremony can be very powerful in stimulating change. Such essences as Rose, Lavender, and White Lotus increase the alchemical process for healing.

As we come closer to true understanding, we become able to receive the medicine that the medicinal essences offer us. Their ancient wisdom conveys immediate results that are both intuitive and practical. They simultaneously ground us and transmit cosmic energy, opening the door for us to receive higher vibrations. I will talk more about this in Chapter 7.

I SENSE: AT PLAY IN THE FIELD OF HEALING

CHAPTER FIVE

A DEEPER DIVE WITH THE DOLPHINS

August 29th, 2008—9:45 pm—Tesuque, New Mexico

With our bags packed, anticipating our morning flight, my wife and I were sound asleep when the phone rang. Jolted awake, I answered with apprehension, knowing this might not be good news. Sure enough, the voice at the other end of the line was the contact for our dolphin boat, saying, "Sam, at this point we have a hurricane watch, and our policy is that we don't cancel unless it's a hurricane warning." My heart sank.

I'd been planning this dolphin swim retreat for almost a year. Twenty-two people were anticipating an amazing trip, but Hurricane Hanna was moving closer to Bimini, Bahamas, throwing a wrench into my well laid-out plans.

"Ok," I replied trying to sound cheerful. "I'll let my group know. See you in Fort Lauderdale." Inside, I was torn. "I must be completely nuts, taking these people into the teeth of a hurricane," I thought, alternating with, "But it's their choice! They want to go." I knew that with the hurricane nearby, we wouldn't be able to get into the ocean. At the same time I had an intuition that it could be a very special trip – just so Hurricane Hanna happened to miss our island.

❖ ❖ ❖ ❖ ❖ ❖ ❖

I often wonder why I have such a strong connection with the Cetacean species.

Growing up, I liked reading books about sea creatures,

especially whales and dolphins. I received great comfort from these stories.

I first learned that dolphins can help us heal during my training in Craniosacral therapy, when I read Dr. John Upledger's research showing that people who received Craniosacral therapy in the water, with dolphins swimming nearby, had very favorable responses. Other scientists' studies showed similar results.

Neuroscientist Dr. John Lilly, in his 20+ years of studies on how humans are affected by being around wild dolphins, found that contact with the dolphins helps improve people's health. Psychologist Dr. David Nathanson's research shows that dolphin interactions with neurologically-impaired children resulted in improved health for many of the children. And British doctor Peter Guy Manners has found that the sounds produced by wild dolphins have a positive therapeutic effect on patients with mental depression and paraplegia.

In popular reports about swimming with dolphins, the interactions often take place in artificial settings. These are not the dolphins I am talking about; these are captive dolphins who have been caught using a drive hunt and forced into an unnatural environment. They are not there by their own choice. Some places that use captive dolphins for entertainment and even for wellness do not treat "their" dolphins very well. Their environments are limited and sterile and can cause the dolphin to sicken or even to die prematurely. I'll say it again: Humans need to learn that we are not entitled to dominate other species, dolphins included.

There is a big difference between spending time with captive dolphins and interacting with wild dolphins. Wild dolphins travel many miles each day, exploring the rich and complex environment of the ocean or river they inhabit. Using a full range of senses, including sonar and other senses that we don't have, they swim and live together with family and friends in close-knit pods. If they spend time with humans, observing or even interacting with us, it is for reasons of their own. Whether because of curiosity, compassion, or for some other reason, these dolphins have chosen to interact with us.

❖ ❖ ❖ ❖ ❖ ❖ ❖ ❖

April 2006, Tesuque, New Mexico and Bimini, Bahamas:

When I was first inspired to take a group to swim with dolphins, I contacted Wildquest. This Bahamas company specializes in human-dolphin interactions, bringing groups out on their catamaran to swim with dolphins in the wild. With one day free in my schedule, I flew all the way from New Mexico to a very small Caribbean island of Bimini, Bahamas, to meet with Amlas, Wildquest's owner. After a two-hour interview, my heart gave me a big yes: The next year, I would bring a group to Bimini for a wellness retreat during which they could interact with wild dolphins. When I announced the idea to my community, people started to sign up immediately. Wow, it was really happening!

And then my ambivalence surfaced. Although I was a good athlete and able swimmer, truth be told, I was afraid of swimming in the open water of the ocean. And here I was, planning to lead a whole group out in the ocean? Further, I was used to working one-on-one in an office, and now I intended to facilitate a group of almost two dozen people. With my tendency to be shy, that was quite a stretch.... But, I told myself, when you get the call, you have to follow it through, and Mother Nature was asking me to do something important. I couldn't turn back.

May 2007, Bimini, Bahamas:

And so my first dolphin group retreat came to be, and twenty-two people with a variety of health issues joined me in the Bahamas for a Wellness Week. During the retreat, we used eye therapy techniques and subtle energy modalities, including color therapy, movement, meditation, and yoga, along with daily swims with the wild Atlantic Spotted Dolphins who are indigenous to that area.

We quickly found that being immersed in the dolphins' field of energy changed our own energy as we became more resonant with ourselves and each other. This increased coherence nurtured us, and I could see that being in the presence of the dolphins

A DEEPER DIVE WITH THE DOLPHINS

was a catalyst for deep healing. When we entered the dolphins' realm, immersing ourselves in their high vibrational state, our low vibrations got stirred up and released. The dolphins' energy field could carry us even when we were not actively engaged with them (reminding me never to underestimate the group energy field). Since dolphin energy is all about open hearts, self-love, playfulness, and sensuality, we awakened to these qualities in ourselves.

Everyone on that retreat suffered from neurological, visual, or other health related issues, some severe, others much less so. And over the course of the trip, all experienced marked improvements in their health pictures. Each day, we spent two hours doing eye-mind-body mindfulness activities. We used primitive reflex movements to relax our reptilian brains and light and color therapy to open our pineal glands. And then we went out on the boat and swam with wild dolphins.

One woman on the retreat had a debilitating spinal and brain abnormality. She gave me permission to share what she wrote about her experience of receiving Craniosacral therapy with dolphins present.

As I entered the water with the dolphins for the first time, the first dolphin I encountered swam right past my head, coming first towards my left side where the worst part of my brain disease is. When experiencing the dolphin assisted Craniosacral session for the first time, I felt an electrical-type surge go through my body. As Dr. Sam started therapy on my spine, the dolphin was swimming across my whole body very slowly, while other dolphins were above and below me. I began to shake and then breathe somewhat heavily. Another dolphin then proceeded to gently lie across my legs for a few seconds. The next day, I experienced this same type of surge, but a little less powerful, while Dr. Sam connected with my spine while the dolphins were circling me. There was also one time when I felt euphoric, as they were above me, around me, and below me, while emitting their echolocation (sound). I could barely move because my body was so relaxed. This therapy brought me great strength in my whole body like I have never felt before. My legs feel incredible and my body is much more limber. I was able to climb up onto the boat without assistance whereas I needed help before the dolphin connections. Overall, I feel more relaxed and at peace. I can definitely do more than I could before I came to this retreat. I am also sleeping much better, and I don't wake up feeling tired. In the morning, I no longer have to wait an hour for my eyes to focus. They have been focusing most mornings without a problem in five minutes.

This first retreat was rewarding and gratifying for me. It gave like-minded people a chance to live in community, as dolphins do, and interact with nature while exploring the idea of "vision" in terms of focus, clarity, intention, and spiritual expansion. The participants experienced holistic health. I decided I wanted to do it again.

❖ ❖ ❖ ❖ ❖ ❖ ❖

August 29, 2008, Fort Lauderdale and Bimini, Bahamas:

Our group came together the next evening at our hotel. A few people had opted out based on the forecasted hurricane, but the rest were there and ready to go. The next morning we awoke early, boarded our little prop plane, and flew to Bimini. According to the hurricane tracker, Hurricane Hanna was due to arrive in three days.

Each day of the retreat, we joined in a circle for a process-oriented session centered on the eyes, vision, and wellness. That first day on the island, as we came together as a group mind, we focused on protecting the islands, the sea creatures, and ourselves from the impending hurricane. The next day, as we watched the weather reports, we were amazed to see that the hurricane seemed to track backwards. And as we watched the tracking on day four, Hanna actually passed to the east of Bimini, missing our retreat altogether. We sat full of wonder and appreciation.

The behavior of the dolphins and their interactions with our group offered us more food for thought that week. Although the seas remained too rough for us to get in the water, pods of dolphins swam around the boat with a level of playfulness and connection that I had not seen before. We could feel the energy they created as they swam with our boat. It was as though they knew we could not join them, and their presence and interaction made it an amazing and life-changing week for our group.

❖ ❖ ❖ ❖ ❖ ❖ ❖

After I returned home and thought about planning the next of these transformational journeys, what came to me was my connection to Hawaii and the energies there. I first went to Hawaii after selling my interests in Philadelphia in 1990. Before settling down in Santa Fe, I headed to Hawaii and spent three weeks hiking and camping around all the islands, and I'd traveled back to Hawaii every year since. Now I realized that if I was going to continue my group dolphin experiences, it would be in those islands and not the Caribbean.

On my dolphin trips to Hawaii, each morning we join together in a circle. I have observed that using essential oils increases our ability to focus our group energy into a coherent pod, so we anoint each other with heart-opening medicinal essences like Carnation, Rose, and Ylang Ylang. Our interactions with the dolphins seem to be even better when we use the essences first, as though they connect with us more easily if we have established a bond with nature to begin with.

The dolphins we interact with on these trips are Hawaiian Spinner Dolphins. Usually, on our first day out, even with the essences we are not yet a coherent group, and the dolphins zap us with a lot of sonar but don't want to stay with us too long. Day 2 usually goes the same way. But by days 3 and 4 we have established a level of coherence and usually have wonderful swims with them.

❖ ❖ ❖ ❖ ❖ ❖ ❖

Through their presence and energy the dolphins can give us messages, if we are open to receive.

One time a wife and husband on the retreat were having conflict. The whole group was aware of it. On day 4, the wife got in the water. She told us later that one dolphin kept swimming with her and beeping with its sonar. It was communicating with her, she said. The message? "Stay with your husband, stay with your husband!" When she shared this with me, I just started laughing. That dolphin was a great marriage counselor, and the woman and her husband healed their disagreement.

I SENSE: AT PLAY IN THE FIELD OF HEALING

On another trip, a man who was dealing with a lot of grief over his father's death was swimming with a dolphin. Dolphins have very sensitive skin and definitely don't want to be touched or to touch us, but that dolphin lightly wacked him three times in the chest area. This behavior seemed extraordinary and I suggested to the man that he should see a doctor to check things out when he returned home. Sure enough, a CAT scan showed a series of small tumors in the lung area. Fortunately, they turned out to be benign. Because subtle energy healing can be an incredibly effective way to bring us back to optimal health, I recommended a protocol of medicinal essential oils to shrink the tumors and help him process his unresolved grief. Three months later, on returning to the doctor, a CAT scan showed that the tumors were totally gone.

A younger couple who came on another trip were processing the pain they experienced because of a miscarriage several months earlier. As we were out swimming one day, a dolphin family – mother, father, and little baby dolphin – approached the pair and they swam and played together for an unusually long time. When the couple returned to the boat, both had tears in their eyes. They told us that the baby dolphin had communicated with them, saying that he was the spirit of the child they had lost and that they shouldn't worry, he was doing really well. They felt reassured and able to begin healing from their loss, and we were all blown away by the depth of this dolphin-human interaction.

❖ ❖ ❖ ❖ ❖ ❖ ❖

I had started working with the GDV camera in 2009 and became intrigued by the idea of measuring peoples' energy fields before and after daily dolphin swims. So, in 2010 and 2011, using the Electrophotonic Imaging Camera under the auspices of its inventor, Dr. Konstantin Korotkov, we performed this research. The results were astonishing. The overall trend was that on the first day, people's energy fields looked jagged and depleted, with small, displaced chakras. But by the fourth day of their swims, the same people's energy fields and chakras were much more coherent than before, more robust, and the participants were sharing these improvements during our evening sessions together.

A DEEPER DIVE WITH THE DOLPHINS

❖ ❖ ❖ ❖ ❖ ❖ ❖

I am fascinated by how our early adaptive patterns subconsciously dominate our adult reactions to life. The impacts of trauma, stress, and toxicity appear time after time in the series of Electrophotonic Imaging pictures taken on day 1, reflecting the state of the group members' fluid systems, fascia, connective tissue, meridians, movement, and vision. But as we become more resonant and open to healing these patterns and our systems get the nourishment we have lacked due to compressions, isolation, and disease states, the images show a very different picture – more robust, vibrant, and in touch, as you can see in the day 4 images. See Chapter 8 to view some of these images.

❖ ❖ ❖ ❖ ❖ ❖ ❖

The fifth eye-opener is that our bio-intelligence is like an umbilical cord connecting us to the cosmos and feeding us. As we begin to connect more deeply to our own fluid vibration, we are also influencing the energy of all beings on the planet.

The dolphins and whales are our friends, inviting us to come into the ocean and swim with them. They use their sonar to see at great distances. As they send their sounds out, they receive the vibration back to themselves and this information flow lets them decide where to go and what to do.

The dolphins are very playful as they spin and twirl, all the while making sounds. They swim in a tetrahedron fashion below us and slowly rise to the surface, giving us eye contact, telling us we are magnificent as we are. Very young dolphins swim and play with their parents. Elder dolphins swim slowly up to us and establish a deep gaze into our eyes.

The dolphins embody fluid movement. As they move with us in spirals we become mesmerized by their dance. Their swimming creates a vortex of energy and as we enter that vortex, our history dissolves and we move out of our normal time-space awareness. On many swims I have lost track of time.

A whole pod might begin to swim around us and we just swim together. Often pods swim very deeply below us, and we hear and feel their sonar all around us. They can vanish and reappear in an instant. If they are busy, we cannot keep up with them.

Dolphins are very calibrated with Mother Earth's energies. If there is a lot of high energy around due to astrological energies or solar flares, they mirror it in their interactions with us. Other times they may swim very slowly, as though they are resting or sleeping, and we share a tranquil and meditative experience.

I love the dolphins' spiraling and twirling movements. Sometimes when I am with them, they swim like silver cylinders deep below me. If they want to play, they may slow down as they surface, making eye contact as we continue to swim together. When they produce bubbles underwater, the bubbles slowly rise to the surface and look like beautiful crystals. Sometimes we play a game where I playfully place my head in the bubbles, and it feels like my brain is absorbing quantum energy produced by the dolphins.

Sometimes, if I meditate after a swim, I receive visions that help me understand the state of the world. The dolphins tell me we should embrace our sensuality and our bodies, using them to move creatively, effortlessly through our lives. They tell me that we need to awaken to a new consciousness which embraces cooperation, community, compassion, playfulness, and, most important of all, love.

The dolphins reflect many of the qualities we humans aspire to embody: unconditional love, harmony, sensuality, play, humor, compassion, wellness, beauty, and grace. They bring us a message of healing ourselves as well as our beautiful Mother Earth. Most of all, the dolphins' message tells us to return to the sea and reconnect to our fluid body of wisdom. As we receive their sound and imitate their spiral movement, we begin to remember our primordial nature as we come into unity/community.

When they want to communicate with us, dolphins use the fluid ocean around them and the fluid inside of us to amplify their voices and sonar, creating a vortex of energy for us to enter. When we do, the lower vibrational memories in our cells and energy field dissipate, and transformation and healing open to us outside our "normal" time-space continuum.

Not only do we take in the dolphins, but also they take us in! Our breathing opens up as we find our own life rhythm. Each time I swim with dolphins, I find myself letting go of our human sense of time. When we enter the dolphins' timeless presence, we can begin to understand the love and unity that are our birthright. They offer us an altered state, free energy, and psychological osmosis.

The dolphins create an energy field that acts as a bridge to take us into other dimensions, helping our brains and bodies to recalibrate to their original patterns of health. They show us how our human connection to all species increases our bio-intelligence for healing, helping us to rediscover our crystalline nature We enter a world where competition, domination, and self-limitation are eliminated. We are birthed into a world of cooperation, unity, and unconditional love.

CHAPTER SIX

FLUID INTELLIGENCE

Water is the foundation of our world, the source of all existence. It connects all living things to each other. Early sea creatures were the original carriers of water. When some moved to the land, they had to find a way to carry the water forward into a new medium. One of water's gifts is how it innately takes the form of its container, and the evolving creatures learned to use water to change form.

Embryos are water beings, almost ninety percent water, and the embryo's DNA is highly influenced by its environment. Waves of communication connect the fetus with its parents, so the fetus is feeling whatever is going on for its parents as strongly as it feels what is going on in utero. These early imprints begin to shape sensory and motor development, as well as social skills and relationship patterns.

Most of us don't inhabit our fluid very well, mainly because we have been taught to ignore our bodies. By plunging into an exploration of the water within us, we have the opportunity to write ourselves a new creation story, to create a new birth-death-birth cycle for ourselves. Why? To deepen our understanding of the meaning of life. By learning about our fluid bodies, we can receive highly enriching fundamental nourishment while gaining access to a heightened state of sensation and pleasure.

Because we are water beings, the fluid body is one of our most potent medicines. One of the keys to personal evolution is being able to connect with and enhance our fluid potency. Once we accomplish this, we can begin to understand an amazing choice each of us is offered – the option of moving beyond our own histories and stories.

❖ ❖ ❖ ❖ ❖ ❖ ❖

Continuum Movement, an incredible healing practice that helps us connect to our own medicine, was invented by Emilie Conrad, a visionary pioneer in the field of somatics. Her groundbreaking work was born as she helped people with spinal cord injuries and other forms of paralysis to regain movement. Emilie was a master, helping people to regain freedom of movement, teaching them to inquire into their fluid bodies with different sequences of sound, breath and spiral movement. Professionals from diverse fields including Rolfing, Zero Balancing, Hellerwork, Craniosacral, osteopathy, and physical therapy all integrate Continuum into their practices.

❖ ❖ ❖ ❖ ❖ ❖ ❖

Most of us don't even know what our bodies are for. The message from today's culture is to train our bodies at the fitness or yoga studio, to restrict our bodies, dominate them, roboticize them, and disconnect from them. Continuum Movement invites us to let go of those messages and, instead, become the master conductors of the symphonies that are our bodies. It invites us to dive into our fluid selves. As we slip into this new way of being, we prepare our fluid bodies to expand and enliven our patterns, behaviors, and tissues. Entering this altered time-space reality, our information flow expands too.

The Continuum revolution is all about breaking away from the synchronized mechanical movements we have been taught. Mechanization keeps our brains locked into rigid patterns of thinking and moving. In order to discover our fluid intelligence, we need to change the repetitive movement patterns so ingrained in us. Diving into our fluid offers us the potential to dissolve and recreate new parts of ourselves, individually and collectively.

When our movements are isolated and repetitive, our bodies become rigid and more compressed, causing problems with everything from movement to eyesight to immunity to emotional balance. Continuum offers a unique healing process that focuses on the fluids in our bodies: blood, cerebral spinal fluid, lymph, and the fluid contained in the muscles and viscera. It teaches that all these fluids work together as one fluid entity, moving in an undulating stream of biological intelligence. In Emilie's words, "The primary characteristic of any fluid system is its ability to keep transforming itself," and the key to Continuum is how it allows us to transform our patterns. She also tells us that learning to inhabit our fluid bodies ignites our own medicine for vibrant health.

❖ ❖ ❖ ❖ ❖ ❖ ❖

As I incorporated Continuum Movement into my practice, I saw my patients learn to recognize how their movement patterns can create closed systems of tension, rigidity, and compression.

For many, these patterns begin in utero when we are just beginning to convert our pre-vertebral tissue to bones. Many of us have a difficult start in life due to stressors during gestation, birth, or infancy. Stressors include negative emotional states in the parents, prenatal exposure to pharmaceutical drugs, unnecessary birthing procedures, and problems with bonding and attachment. These and other difficult situations can set the stage for us to adapt a habitual unconscious survival response.

With Continuum, watching our breath and following the movement in our body container, we gain much more oxygenation. As we let go of the need for our survival responses, we start to see our levels of pain, illness, and emotional stress decrease.

As we become aware of our bodies' fluids, the health of our nervous systems begins to change. We connect to the potency of the fluid body which arises much further upstream in our prenatal development. The Continuum formula helps to heal pre-natal patterns that can affect us well into adulthood.

Continuum helps us to slow down and sense the body, following our impulses and rhythms in the moment, letting go of control. The responsiveness of our bodies is a direct measurement of our health, vitality, and overall energy flow. The more we are able to relax into this new mode, the more we can connect with the natural rhythms which help us to recharge and become nourished. Since our bodies know exactly what we need, if we slow down, listen, and follow, we will connect to our innate wisdom for healing, rejuvenation, and renewal.

❖ ❖ ❖ ❖ ❖ ❖ ❖

Sound, Breath, and Movement: Three Ingredients in Continuum Movement

Sound

One of Continuum's most important tools is the use of self-created sound to vibrate the tissues. The gentle vibration helps shake loose the tension that our patterned tissues hold in place. Our beautiful sounds and tones increase inner harmony, making it easier to return to our fluid source. Emilie discovered that different sounds activate different tissues: there is a sound for the bones, another for the bone marrow, another which activates our immune system. There are sounds that create lateral spread of the tissues and others that elongate the tissues. The more modulation we have in our sound, the more versatility we can access in our fluid, giving us more resources to draw from.

One common imprint from childhood has to do with "being seen but not heard." Often, workshop participants are very shy about making sounds. When they finally do make a sound, I encourage them to use this stimulus to observe the movement of the tissue. Our compressed areas love sound it helps them to communicate with each other in a more communal way. When tissue flow is compressed because of stress, toxicity, or trauma, sound helps the area to relax and expand, restoring the flow of information with both our inner and outer environments, a key element in the nourishing the body's systems.

Breath

Breath is another major component of Continuum. Our breathing patterns carry the imprint of the first breaths we took at birth. If we experienced distress in those first breaths, we carry that imprint. We learned our early breathing patterns from our mothers, and if those patterns were restricted, we carry that imprint. In Continuum

I SENSE: AT PLAY IN THE FIELD OF HEALING

Movement, we focus on our breathing instead of our thoughts or emotions. We learn to track and observe the level and scope of our breathing, noticing the movement of the diaphragm. Restricted breathing causes lack of movement in the body, shrinking the tissues and reducing our flow of information. The sounds we make in Continuum help deepen the breath inherently, from the inside out.

As we practice Continuum, we become more connected with our breathing baseline. At the beginning of a Continuum dive, we ask ourselves the following questions: Do we breathe deeply? What is the quality of our breathing? What is the speed of our breathing? Are we mouth breathers?

When I started doing Continuum, I discovered that my inhalation-exhalation was very shallow and fast. I was breathing faster than I could ever move my body. This pattern is typical of the fight or flight response, and I could feel that it created body compression and tissue starvation. As I slowed my breathing, I could feel the new movement it created within my body container. I felt empowered to recognize and change this habit.

Breathing through the mouth rather than the nose puts us in a hyperventilation mode. When I teach Continuum, I regularly ask my clients to bond with their breathing cycle instead of bonding with their mind's mental somersaults. When a person is able to do this, it becomes possible to renew one's energy flow.

Observing our breath teaches the connection between inhalation and exhalation, which is a birth and death cycle. As we slow and deepen our breathing, our tissues spread, allowing more nourishment, softening our resistance to gravity. We start to feel the wind (breath) over the water (our fluid body). Breath is spirit.

Movement

The third component of Continuum is movement. In Continuum, we move our bodies in a spiral, wave, or pulsation. As we become more aware of our inherent fluid nature, we connect to our own wave potential. As we let go of the tension, over-focusing, and speed that narrow our sensory attention, our tissue begins to open. Each in our own context, we can begin to reduce the conformity that is present in our bodies. As we soften and spread, we notice that our fluid is moving us. The movements become even more subtle and we begin to be able to resonate with our own innate rhythms. The more we deepen, the softer our survival circuits become. We become able to soften our identity. At the core, we find ourselves completely honoring our own rhythms rather than conforming to follow others.

One of the aspects I explore concerning movement is called biological tensegrity. Structures such as tendons, ligaments, bones, muscles, and fascia are both rigid and elastic. Although they are made strong by the unison of tensioned and compressed parts, they are comprised mostly of fluid. As we refine our movements, we can sense a very delicate but expansive shape shifting in our body. As the fluid becomes more coherent, it moves the tissue in undulating ways that return us to our origins as sea creatures. How we move is how we think, how we think is how we move, and this all has a profound effect on our interpersonal relationships and life itself.

Open attention

Open Attention, another important aspect of Continuum, gives us an opportunity to inquire into how our breathing and sounding affect our movement and, ultimately, our fluid health. We spend so much time in the busy state of doing, and Open Attention invites us to just be and receive the nourishment we have been lacking. Open Attention rekindles the parasympathetic nervous system, which helps with healing, purification, and rejuvenation. After completing a sequence of breath, sound, and movement practice, we practice Open Attention. Can we listen deeply to tissue and honor its movement?

Group energy

Continuum is usually done in a group setting, creating a very rich, high vibration group consciousness and energy field, effortlessly amplifying the healing energy for all who are present.

❖ ❖ ❖ ❖ ❖ ❖ ❖

Once we connect with our breathing, we develop greater

somatic intelligence becoming more willing to take responsibility for ourselves. We no longer need to blame "it" out there. We become aware of our somatic inheritance and how much of our body patterning is passed through the morphogenetic field into our own echo of awareness.

Environmental factors influence our genes' expression, affecting vision, mobility, breath, and overall sensory functions and behavior. In order for awakening to occur, we need to become aware of our patterns. Continuum can help us learn to regulate ourselves so we depend on our own healing power, and not on doctors, drugs, or surgery. In fact, most Continuum practitioners are able to take their clients much farther along in their healing, because the practitioners themselves continue to play at the edge of their own healing.

❖ ❖ ❖ ❖ ❖ ❖ ❖

Movement stimulates our seeing, seeing stimulates our movement.

Many times, when I apply Continuum Movement to peoples' eyes and vision, they start to recognize eye-mind-body patterns caused by repetitive focusing tasks, such as those that occur when using a computer, tablet, or smart phone. The visual confinement caused by these repeated patterns may result in deterioration in the eye tissue, and while we may interpret that deterioration as a sign of aging, it's really caused by a lack of nutrients in tissue that requires a nutrient-rich environment to thrive. Corrective lenses only embed the pattern, further disconnecting the users from their sensations.

Sixth eye opener: The eyes are made up of some of the most unrealized tissue of the body. When we focus them for any length of time at one distance, a closed system of movement is set up. Closed systems solidify the fluids in the eye tissue, creating and becoming a dead zone. The lymph, cerebrospinal fluid, and blood that pass through the eyes lock down due to this closed system, especially when using electronics. Continuum and Craniosacral therapies help people regain the fluid nature of their eyes.

My declaration is to Occupy Our Eyes and Our Bodies, Fully!

❖ ❖ ❖ ❖ ❖ ❖ ❖

Sensation Versus Emotion

The psychotherapeutic model, in my estimation, is in need of an upgrade. Too many therapists appear to believe that the way to heal our traumas is to re-experience them. This re-wounding or re-stimulation of the past can cause us to become addicted to emotional release, but does little to actually heal the trauma.

Repeatedly re-experiencing our historic emotions takes us out of our first order of experience, causing us to base our orientation on our history rather than on what is going on right now in our bodies and our lives. The freedom we experience by staying with sensation is profound.

❖ ❖ ❖ ❖ ❖ ❖ ❖

Continuum helps us connect to a different technology – a biological technology. One of the practices I propose is a return to the spirit of water. Water, with its primal nature, knows no boundaries. It is the magical, the alchemical substance where the medicine exists.

Water spirit tells us that we are connected to all fluid in the universe - fluid in the trees in the form of essential oils, fluid of the embryo, and fluid in the galaxies. The more we connect to these fractals, the more we connect to coherence. As we open to a larger field, we increase our potential to receive nourishment and replenishment.

The fluid energy field carries memory and information not only of this individual life. It also carries the history of billions of years of planetary intelligence. This is what we access as we dive into our fluid body.

CHAPTER SEVEN

THE WISDOM
SCHOOL OF NATURE

N.D.D.

Mother Earth is doing everything she can to get our attention. She is wreaking havoc with extreme weather events like earthquakes, floods, droughts, hurricanes, and wildfires. The nuclear catastrophe at Fukushima is posing a major ecological threat for the entire Pacific basin and, ultimately, for the entire ecosystem of Planet Earth.

Each of us has the option take three steps before we can help our planet to heal:

— First, we must first recognize our condition: N.D.D., or Nature Deficit Disorder.

— Second, we must realize that we are not the pinnacle of evolution. We like to see ourselves as the dominant species, but we vastly over-rate our role.

— And third, we must recognize that our over-worked left brains have disconnected us from Mother Earth and her resources.

Once we have taken these steps, our species may be able to transcend our survival response and enter a state of coherence, love, and unity. Then, if it's not too late, we can join together in global planetary service.

❖ ❖ ❖ ❖ ❖ ❖ ❖

By making it personal, we can each develop our own connection with Nature and find the deep care, healing, and wisdom that she offers.

FLUID INTELLIGENCE

"In this process of unlearning, in the process of feeling and hearing the plants again, one comes to realize many things. And of these things, perhaps stronger than the others, one feels the pain of the Earth. It is not possible to escape it.

One of the most powerful experiences I had of this was the year when I traveled to the Florida panhandle. One day Trishuwa and I decided to go out and make relationship with the plants and offer prayer to them. The place we chose appeared quite lush, with huge trees and thick undergrowth. But as we sat there, a strong anger came from the land and the trees. They had little use for us and told us so in strong language. We spoke with them for a long time and did not cower away from their rage and eventually, as we received their pain and anger, they calmed down a little. They told us that we could do our ceremonies if we wished and that they appreciated the thought but that it would do no good. It was too late for that place, it could not be helped, the land would take its revenge for the damage done to it and nothing would stop it. I wondered then how everyone who lived in the area could just go on with their daily lives when this communication from all the local living things was crying out so loudly. I wondered if anyone else felt this rage and anger."

—Stephen Harrod Buhner,
Sacred Plant Medicine: The Wisdom in Native American Herbalism
http://www.goodreads.com/author/quotes/90999.Stephen_Harrod_Buhner

The Plants and Trees inspire me to deepen my connection with myself and others. Maybe you'll think I'm crazy if I tell you that the spirits of the essences speak to me. Or, if you too are a seeker of a similar kind, maybe you will understand when I say what a gift it is that these devas honor me with their wisdom. They tell me that I am a messenger, carrying knowledge from the natural world to each person I reach. In this chapter, I have the honor of sharing their wisdom with you.

Wisdom of the Earth Medicinal Essences

Barry Kapp, founder of the medicinal essence company Wisdom of the Earth and author of *Wisdom of The Earth Speaks*, has said during his workshops that, the Plant and Tree Kingdom share their wisdom with us via medicinal essences. They remind us to live in our hearts not only on a physical 3D level, but also in our morphogenetic fields, so that our love and reverence for Mother Gaia can be realized. The more we trust the information that the Plants and Trees convey to us, the more we connect to our intuition – which tells us, "Choose the love paradigm!" I agree with Barry, but I have to wonder: Can we sit with the idea that we can change the direction of our evolution?

Rollin McCraty, Ph.D., the Executive Vice President and Director of Research at the Institute of HeartMath helped to organize the Global Coherence Initiative. This science-based, co-creative project helps unite people in heart-focused care and intention, to facilitate the shift in global consciousness from instability and discord to balance, cooperation, and enduring peace. In their research, they have found that greater personal coherence improves global coherence and social harmony and empowers environmental responsibility and stewardship of our planet.

I have developed a few hypotheses that I have been exploring in my own research with medicinal essential oils and healing. Here are a few of them:

1. All living things are interrelated and interconnected.
2. All living things communicate through both biological and electromagnetic fields.
3. All living things can both affect and be affected by planetary energetic fields, the Earth's magnetic fields, and our natural world.
4. If all living things can broadcast love, compassion, and gratitude, these thought forms can offset the current incoherence and stress waves that surround us.

Both magnetic and bio-energetic fields affect our body rhythms, which include our heart rate, breathing pattern, fluid resonance, nervous system and our brain waves. As we come together in a group, our coherence is magnified.

How To Use Essences

I can't say strongly enough how important it is to use only the highest quality pure medicinal essences, and those made by Wisdom of the Earth are the best I've been able to find, with the highest vibration possible for healing and spiritual growth. I have observed how deeply they address our deeper emotional, spiritual, and physical connection to ourselves, all other species, and Mother Earth. In fact I feel so strongly about these products that I teach aromatherapy using Wisdom of the Earth products.

Because it is important to maintain the most intimate relationship possible with the Plants and Trees during the growing, harvesting and processing of the essences, these essences are all hand-poured in ceremony. No machines are used anywhere in the equation.

❖ ❖ ❖ ❖ ❖ ❖ ❖

Seventh Eye Opener: Medicinal essences are the blood of Plants and Trees.

I have been using medicinal essences to convey the Plant and Tree Kingdom's wisdom to my brothers and sisters. They have many lessons to teach us. When I ask about their needs, the Plants and Trees respond that we should acknowledge that they are our elders and treat them with respect and reverence, and that we are here to steward the other species and Mother Earth.

The more we can open to this type of relationship, the higher our vibration will be and the more health, wellness, love, and peace we can broadcast, (omit comma) to ourselves and to others. When we can trust, feel, and express with our hearts, we will be able to communicate exactly what is needed to complete the circle of love.

What we get from essences

Of the 4.56 billion years of Earth's life, we have only been here a few hundred thousand years. The Plants and Trees remind us that we are only one part of a diverse ecosystem, and if we stop trying to dominate all other species, we may be able to heal ourselves and Mother Earth.

These powerful essences humbly teach that our human species can transcend its superiority problem. They offer many opportunities to connect heart-to-heart, to slow down, listen, and follow their instructions and guidance, and to reconnect with Earth Mother. For example, we can use flower essences from Neroli, Jasmine, and Rose to help us return to our hearts and soften our entitled attitudes.

The Plants and Trees tell us that we need to have a deeper connection to Mother Earth. They offer to help soften our fixed, rigid points of view. They say we should take responsibility for the healing we receive through the essences.

The Plant and Tree Kingdom offers wisdom to humans. They ask us to sit at their feet and allow them to teach what they know so well. I recommend that you offer yourself to the Plants and Trees and see what they have to say to you.

❖ ❖ ❖ ❖ ❖ ❖ ❖

These are some teachings that the essences have imparted to me:

— Medicinal essences, especially pure unadulterated essences, open and connect us to other dimensions.
— Medicinal essences soften the ego's attempt to attach to and control others.
— Medicinal essences beckon us to live in our hearts, not our minds and egos, and connect us to our spirit self (God-self). Remember, EGO stands for "Edge God Out."
— Medicinal essences offer a complexity that connects us to a higher vibration and frequency.
— Some medicinal essences are more Yin (cooling, female) and some are more Yang (warming, male). When we use them we reunite our own masculine-feminine energies to a united consciousness.
— Medicinal essences show us that abundance means much more than accumulating on the material plane.
— Medicinal essences assist in planetary service and will help create a new civilization.
— Medicinal essences help us remember who we are and how we can support the nature spirits in doing their job.

— Medicinal essences can teach us about spiritual mastery.
— Medicinal essences teach us about vibrational healing, returning to our birthright as creator-beings.
— Medicinal essences help awaken us to a deeper connection to Mother Earth and to spiritual as well as physical and emotional healing.
— When used with a group, medicinal essences unify and amplify the energy connections in the field, bringing about healing.
— Medicinal essences remind us that we are spiritual beings in human bodies.
— Medicinal essences show us about free energy.
— Medicinal essences help us jump timelines.
— Medicinal essences are biological technologies that create a quantum field effect.

❖ ❖ ❖ ❖ ❖ ❖ ❖

Specific essences and their messages:

Different plants offer different parts of themselves to us through their essences. These are some of the metaphorical messages we can receive by using different plant parts on a daily basis:

These SEEDS help us bring forth new ideas:
Sweet Fennel, Cumin Seed, Ambrette Seed

These WOODS help us with gentle but fierce resiliency:
Sandalwood, Rosewood

These ROOTS remind us to ground ourselves in Mother Earth:
Angelica Root, Vetiver, Ginger

These BARKS offer us protection and strength:
Birch, Red Spruce, Cinnamon Bark

These RESINS help our glandular, respiratory, and immune systems find harmony. They help us access peace, quiet, and stillness:
Elemi, Myrrh, Galbanum

These FLOWERING TOPS guides us to unconditional self-love and balancing the nervous system:
Lavender, Hyssop

These LEAVES AND NEEDLES help us convert our food into energy so we have the resources to connect with the seasons and rhythms of life. They also help us to clarify any cloudiness in our lives:
Eucalyptus, Pettigrains, Fir

These WHOLE FRUITS helps us take new information and synthesize it:
Black Pepper, Clove Bud

These FRUIT PEELS support the fluid part of ourselves to express our movement with gusto and innovation!
Lemon, Lime, Mandarin

These FLOWERS help us connect to the sensuality, creativity, and beauty in our life. They ask us to connect to our own essence (the nectar) and spread that love everywhere, to be open to all healthy collaborations and making relations!
Rose, Ylang Ylang, Jasmine

DECIDUOUS TREES remind us to learn and embody the cycles of life. These trees drop their leaves and go to sleep for the winter, then are reborn in the spring. Can we connect and follow the cycles of life?

CONIFEROUS TREES help us connect to the cosmos, the stars, and the realization that we are not alone in the universe. They remind us that star seed relations are here to help us transition to a higher vibration of consciousness.

❖ ❖ ❖ ❖ ❖ ❖ ❖

Over the years, certain essences have spoken to me about how they can support us on our journeys to connect and integrate our physical worlds with our spiritual selves. Here is what they had to say:

WHITE LOTUS: "Humans are in the right place at the right time. The more they can heal their relationship with the money elemental, the more the flow of life will come to them."

BASIL EXOTICA: "I am very sturdy. I am here to support humans embracing their strength and endurance on an energetic plane."

RED PINE: "Use my root system to experience the interconnectedness of all life."

SPRUCE NORWAY "As life change intensifies, my resiliency is yours to access."

GINGER: "I am here to help process and digest your past and present and prepare you for the future."

VIOLET: "The soft beauty I offer will help your children find the courage to feel their aliveness and creativity."

TEA TREE: "I am here to give supreme health. Use me to improve and support your dental health."

FRANKINCENSE: "My versatility helps you transform cancer patterns on all levels."

INDIAN LEMONGRASS: "My warm embrace cuts through resistance and inspires new forms of consciousness to be born."

SWEET MARJORAM: "Remember your ancestors. They offer guidance on navigating our evolution."

❖ ❖ ❖ ❖ ❖ ❖ ❖

Some of my go-to essences:

SPIKENARD amplifies and expands our dream world and protects our energy field from the skin to the aura.

GERANIUM encourages balance and connects our inner and outer light.

GOLDENROD reminds us of the abundance we forget about. She is here to say, open your heart, feel the radiance that is inside of us!

NARCISSUS tells us to be fierce and gentle about loving and being loved. Rise above resistance and ego. Connect to ourselves and others will connect to themselves.

ROSE is about the love vibration. She will teach us about loving ourselves like no other and will support us through any trial and tribulation. We have to add our trust to this equation.

CHAMPACA helps with grounding ourselves in Mother Earth with grace, lightness, and truth. She shows us that the veils are very thin.

SAFFRON says, open your eyes and see. But the deeper question to ask is, "Are you ready to see it all and see it clearly?" She does not mince words. Her Yang energy is about burning off the resistance and staying the course.

PALO SANTO says, I am grounding so deeply into Mother Earth, and the deeper I go, the more exhilarated I feel. Get down and dirty, because that is what is needed to make the changes we need.

❖ ❖ ❖ ❖ ❖ ❖ ❖

Medicinal essences, combined with Color Therapy in the eyes and sound healing using Tibetan bowls or tuning forks, are a wonderful tool for Chakra balancing. Here is a list of essences I use in my Chakra balancing workshops:

ROOT CHAKRA: Juniper Berry teaches us how to be resourceful! She is the Queen of the Autonomic Nervous System.

SECOND CHAKRA: Siberian Fir Needle is about being sensual and connecting to our own sexuality. She helps us increase pleasure and boosts our energy and immune system.

THIRD CHAKRA: Ginger teaches how to work with our ego identity, and at the same time help us connect deeply to our personal power. She is the Queen of Digestion.

FOURTH CHAKRA: Ylang Ylang shows us how to increase our love and compassion. This beautiful flower asks us to practice unconditional love with ourselves.

FIFTH CHAKRA Laurel Leaf helps us to speak our truth and talk about our passion. She protects our energy field. She is the Queen of the Lymph System.

SIXTH CHAKRA: Spikenard helps us to be more intuitive, increases our psychic vision, and helps us see into the unseen world. If you want to explore your dreams, use six drops of Spikenard on the top of the head before bed. She will take you places you have not been before.

SEVENTH CHAKRA: White Spruce helps us connect with unity consciousness and helps us develop our own expression with truth and faith. She also helps us connect to our grandfather and grandmother ancestors.

❖ ❖ ❖ ❖ ❖ ❖ ❖

Using Essences with Animals

I mentioned my colleague Tresa Laferty in Chapter 5. A gifted animal communicator and aromatherapist, Tresa teaches that spirit comes into certain beings to enable them to have the experience of living as domesticated animals, and that we as humans can

I SENSE: AT PLAY IN THE FIELD OF HEALING

help animals in that experience. Dogs, for example, have become pleasing, social family pets that are required to fit into people's ideas of how they should be. If we recognize that dogs need to have their own journey, we can use medicinal essences to help them along their way.

❖ ❖ ❖ ❖ ❖ ❖ ❖ ❖

The Field of Aromatherapy

Depending on what you read and who you talk to, you may have heard arguments about whether aromatherapy, or any use of medicinal essences, is valid, useful, or scientific. If we look at medicinal aromatherapy only through our left brains, we will spend a lot of time conducting double blind studies and gas chromatograms and graphing the results and comparing the studies.... Meanwhile, our right brains are drawn to the emotional, spiritual, gestalt being in our hearts, wanting to leap in and trust the medicine that the essences have to offer.

I live in both the left-brain and right-brain worlds and have observed that the more we allow ourselves to take in the essences, the more they take us in. This synergistic relationship allows the essences to work at deep spiritual levels and not just physically, on a symptomatic level. The more we surrender to the Plant and Tree Kingdom, the healthier we can be. As we let go of our need to see humans as superior, we can discover the power of being connected to a species-inclusive consciousness.

I define medicinal aromatherapy as the original medicine of the earth. The medicinal essences are based on pure love, not fear. They are very alive and bring us harmony and peace. They help us tap into our own life force, opening doors of possibilities, bringing renewed energy, and creating new paradigms of thinking (from their perspective as well as ours).

Fear has created a lot of misinformation about using medicinal essences. We have to remember the essential truth that it is part of our birthright to connect to our own biology for healing, transformation, and aliveness!

I SENSE: AT PLAY IN THE FIELD OF HEALING

CHAPTER EIGHT

STRENGTHENING OUR WELL-BEING: FINE-TUNING TO THE NATURAL RHYTHMS OF LIFE

The eighth eye opener: "When thine eye is single, the body is full of light."

Luke 11:34

As a holistic practitioner, behavioral optometrist, teacher, researcher, and scientist, I have observed great improvements in peoples' health using my wellness program. One of the main threads in my approach is that the eyes reveal many of our mind-body patterns related to health. For example, neuroscience shows that the eye pathway connects directly to and influences brain function, the endocrine system, and the nervous system. Somatics reveals that prenatal infant movements affect adult postural, visual, and cognitive patterns. Chinese medicine says that many of the energy meridians connect to the eyes, especially the liver (our major detoxification organ).

I like to use an individualized approach, guiding each person to self-discover the visual patterns and imprints they use as an adaptive response to stress, trauma, and cultural conditioning. Using a developmental process of eye-brain awareness activities, somatic movement, medicinal essential oils, and subtle energy therapies, I help people connect to their own bio-intelligence for health.

I also have found that the group dynamic or unified field amplifies healing. By holding a space of gentle, humorous energy, I offer people a safe, trusting environment for healing. Here they can discover their own wellness potential and develop a sustained health practice that incorporates deeper self-responsibility and self-regulation.

I have researched a variety of disciplines with respect to expanding human potential. These include Vision Therapy, biofield analysis, light therapy, Continuum Movement, medicinal essential oils, and dolphin-assisted therapy.

Below are a few studies I have done using the GDV camera as the research tool to test this question: do these modalities have an effect on the biofield?

And my second question: if the biofield is affected, does this change influence our wellness?

Biofield Measurements

The GDV Biofield Analysis provides a graphic image of the physical, emotional, and spiritual energy fields and chakras. According to Dr. Korotkov's GDV research, the energy fields are comprised of electrical, electromagnetic, and subtle energies that support our vitality and wellness. Toxicities, traumas, inflammation, and stress can all be imprinted onto the energy field. Spikes, spaces, unevenness, or jaggedness in the energy field all indicate imprints that are affecting our physical, emotional, psychological, and spiritual health. Part of the biofield analysis also includes the size and alignment of the seven major chakras. These are subtle energy channels that feed different glands, organs, nerves, and fluids and show the degree of energy flow surrounding the body

My first study was using a medicinal essential oils protocol on a patient suffering a bladder infection. After two weeks of antibiotics, she was still experiencing pain when urinating. I recommended a protocol using the following essences: Sandalwood, Rose, Cistus, and Helichrysum Immortelle in a tampon, and applying it twice a day, once for 6 hours and once before bedtime. She did the treatment for one week.

I SENSE: AT PLAY IN THE FIELD OF HEALING

Figure 1 shows the left energy field to be spikey and ragged. Figure 2 shows her second and third chakras out of alignment. Her second chakra is shifted right of midline, indicating that she is giving her sexuality and power away to others. Her third chakra is shifted left of midline, which means that she had lost connection with her own personal power—especially within feminine expression. She responded to this by telling me that she really needed to end the relationship with her boyfriend but was afraid to confront him.

After using the essential oil protocol, she came back for a second measurement. In figure 3, the left field is brighter and more even. In figure 4, the chakras are aligned. Her report was that, when her primary care doctor did another culture, the bacterial infection was gone. So was her pain. She shared that she had joined a women's circle and was developing more of her feminine expression.

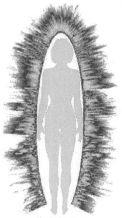

Subject 1. Capture 1 (no filter)

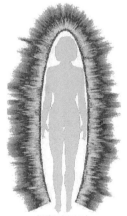

Subject 1, Capture 1 (filter)

Fig. 1

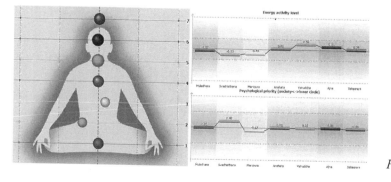

Fig. 2

95

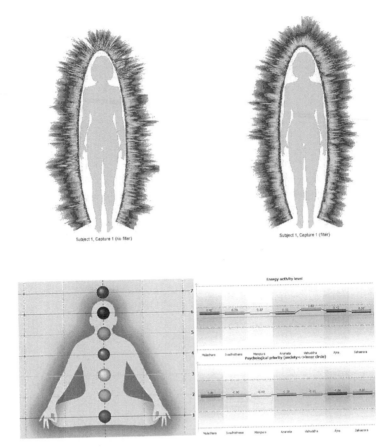

Fig. 3

Subject 1, Capture 1 (no filter)   Subject 1, Capture 1 (filter)

Fig. 4

Craniosacral Study

In 2010 while teaching a workshop at the Esalen Institute, I performed a Craniosacral Therapy study to see if one treatment would affect the biofield.

I asked a Craniosacral therapist to perform a 1.25 hour session on one of the participants from my group.

The woman who received the treatment was rear-ended at a stoplight, two weeks before the workshop. The left side of her body was in pain, especially in the lower thoracic and lumbar areas of the spine. She was still very upset by the accident. In Figure 1, the left field shows more shock and trauma versus the right side of the body. In Figure 2, the second through fifth chakras are right

I SENSE: AT PLAY IN THE FIELD OF HEALING

of midline and very small. When she saw this configuration, she shared that her car was hit on the left side, and that her pain was on that side. When the chakras are on the right side, this means that a person is looking for others to help. She had seen many therapists to help her heal from this accident.

I measured her 30 minutes after the Craniosacral treatment. In Figure 3, the field on the left side looks more filled in, but still jagged and disorganized. I interpreted the picture as someone in the process of taking in new information from the treatment and integrating it into the body. In Figure 4, the chakras have increased in size and come into alignment except for the third chakra. She had an emotional release while being treated, and recognized that the position of the third chakra represented her unresolved feelings about the driver. She felt much more relaxed and her pain had decreased by about 75%.

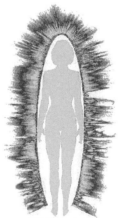 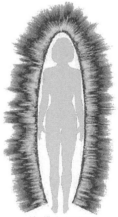

Subject 1(1), Capture 1 (no filter)   Subject 1(1), Capture 1 (filter)

Fig. 1

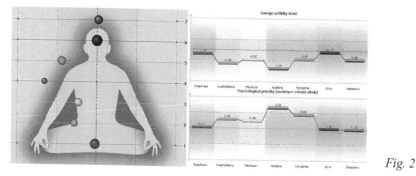

Fig. 2

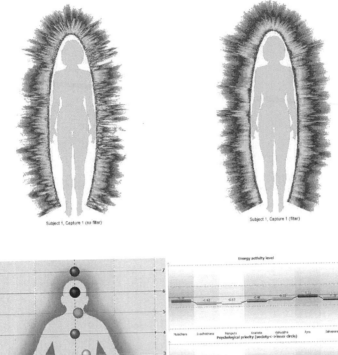

Fig. 3   Subject 1, Capture 1 (no filter)   Subject 1, Capture 1 (filter)

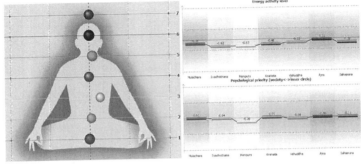

Fig. 4

Continuum Movement Study

During my early studies of Continuum, I participated in a five day retreat led by Emilie Conrad, the practice's founder, at her studio in Santa Monica. I agreed to measure one of the participants, a 53 year old male, before and after the retreat to see if Continuum Movement could change the biofield. Figure 1 shows his energy field before the retreat began. The left field has some holes and is very jagged. In Figure 2, the second and fifth chakras are very small and the fifth chakra is left of midline. This configuration suggests that the person is not connecting to his voice. Also, both the first and fourth chakras are left of midline. This picture says he is not connecting to himself around issues related to grounding and self-

I SENSE: AT PLAY IN THE FIELD OF HEALING

love. Figure 3 shows a measurement taken 15 minutes after the end of the retreat. The left field is much more filled in and the spikes around the throat suggest some reconnection to his voice. In Figure 4, all the chakras are aligned and the throat chakra has increased in size. The man shared that he felt so alive and connected after the retreat. He felt that he had healed the childhood pattern of "you can be seen but not heard." He loved the sounds that he was able to explore in Continuum.

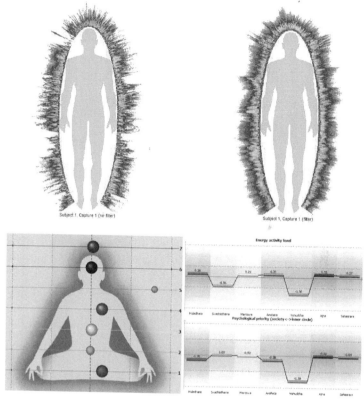

Fig. 1

Fig. 2

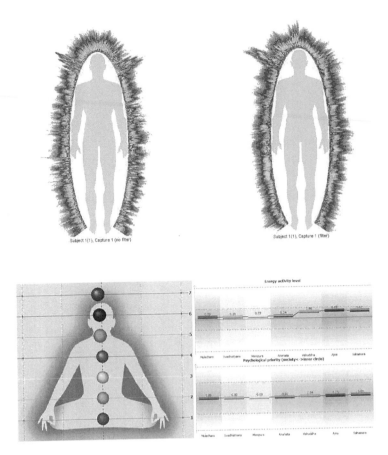

Fig. 3

Subject 1(1), Capture 1 (no filter)

Subject 1(1), Capture 1 (filter)

Fig. 4

Light Therapy Study

At another retreat at Esalen, I treated a group of people using a light/color machine employing the Rainbow method. In this treatment, people sit together, while a light machine projects colors for 30 seconds each, in a sequence starting with the red end of the spectrum and ending at indigo violet. I ask the participants to describe the body sensations they felt while looking at each color. The treatment takes 20 minutes to complete.

I measured one person as the group's the energetic representative. (This works because in a group experience, the participants form a unified field and share energy readily with each other.)

In Figure 1, the left energy field looks ragged and has some holes in it. In Figure 2, the chakras are scattered and look very

100   I SENSE: AT PLAY IN THE FIELD OF HEALING

small. Generally, when the chakras are on the left side, they reflect private or personal reality. When the chakras are drifted to the right side, we are being asked to explore our issues that are part of a community or public reality.

After waiting five minutes I re-measured her biofield. In Figure 3, the biofield looks brighter and smoother, and although there are still holes, they are in a different place. The picture shows that she is in a process of integrating the new energetic information. In Figure 4, the chakras look lined up. The light therapy influenced her chakra size and alignment. Not only did she feel more centered, balanced, and relaxed, the group as a whole felt the same way after this session.

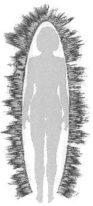 

Fig. 1

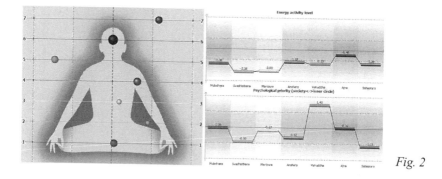

Fig. 2

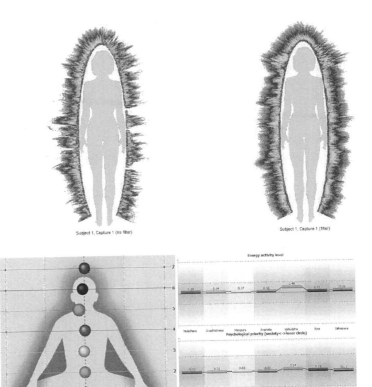

Fig. 3

Subject 1, Capture 1 (no filter)

Subject 1, Capture 1 (filter)

Fig. 4

Dolphin Swim Retreat 2010 Kona Hawaii

In this study, I measured people the evening before the first dolphin swim and three hours after the last dolphin swim. In Figure 1, before the first swim, the person's energy field shows many holes as well as shock and trauma. In Figure 2, the chakra alignment is disorganized, especially in the upper chakra area. In Figure 3, after the last swim, the energy fields are brighter with less holes. In Figure 4, the chakras are aligned. The participant shared that the dolphin retreat helped her heal from old child sexual abuse. She shared that she felt more hopeful in her life than at the beginning of the retreat. She also felt that her work was about healing her feminine expression.

I SENSE: AT PLAY IN THE FIELD OF HEALING

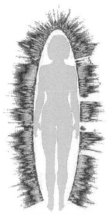
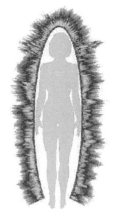

Subject 1, Capture 1 (no filter)

Subject 1, Capture 1 (filter)

Fig. 1

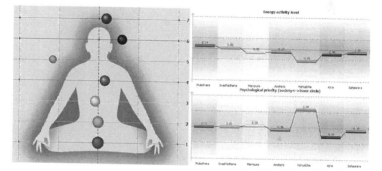

Fig. 2

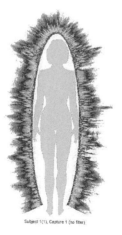
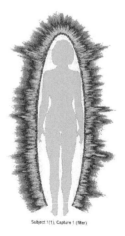

Subject 1(1), Capture 1 (no filter)

Subject 1(1), Capture 1 (filter)

Fig. 3

STRENGTHENING OUR WELL-BEING

103

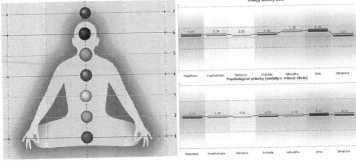

Fig. 4

Raymond's Story

A few years ago, the parent's of a six-year-old who had been diagnosed with Asperger's Syndrome called me for a consultation. I am including his case study here because, in addition to illustrating the changes that holistic modalities create in the biofield, it also offers a greater glimpse into my use of these treatments.

1. Case History

"Raymond" is a six-year-old diagnosed with Asperger's Syndrome. His medical history showed:
- Prenatal: stressful
- Birth: C-section
- Early Childhood: colic with ear infections
- Medications: none
- Developmental History: never crawled

In other parts of his history he:
- Appears lost in his own world
- Lacks eye contact
- Hypersensitive to touch and noise
- Shows anger and aggressiveness
- Exhibits stimming (repetitive stereotypic) behavior
- Does not finish tasks
- Odd speech pattern
- Disorganized, messy room

I performed three evaluations on Raymond:
- A Tissue Mineral Analysis
- GDV Biofield Analysis
- A Developmental-Visual-Learning Assessment

Tissue Evaluation Results

The Tissue Mineral Analysis showed imbalances in his carbohydrate metabolism (calcium-magnesium ratio), adrenal burnout (sodium-potassium ratio), poor dietary absorption (high phosphorous in his test results), and high heavy metal levels (lead, mercury, arsenic, and aluminum).

(See Figures 1 and 2) Overall, Raymond's initial energy patterns reflect that he is functioning in a very depleted state. The holes in his biofield show that Raymond is locked into the "freeze" state (reptilian response). These holes represent trauma imprints from his C-section birth. Spaces in this part of the biofield indicate that his energy is not flowing equally throughout the body. Influences that we refer to as "entities" may enter these holes and negatively influence Raymond's behavior and emotions. Raymond's soul's expression is severely compromised. Allopathic medicine would call this Autism. Fortunately, Raymond's parents had the

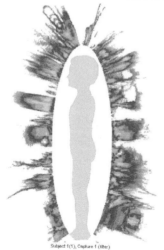

Subject 1(1), Capture 1 (filter)

Subject 1, Capture 1 (no filter)

Before Treatment.
Notice spaces in the field.
Figure 1

Biofield before Treatment
Notice all the spaces in the field
Figure 2

STRENGTHENING OUR WELL-BEING

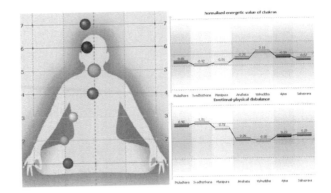

Chakras
Before Treatment
Figure 3

consciousness to understand the distinction between an allopathic diagnosis versus an analysis of his biofield.

(See Figure 3) In this picture, the lower three chakras are floating to Raymond's right side, which means that he is giving his power away to others in his root, his sexuality, and his power centers. He is also giving his power away in his third eye and his spiritual center. The throat chakra is unusually large, indicating that he is trying to compensate for these misalignments through his throat chakra.

Developmental-Visual-Learning Assessment

Raymond showed significant developmental delays in all of his sensory motor systems, his primitive reflexes, and birth trauma.

Treatment Protocol

Because Raymond was suffering from shock and trauma as well as biochemical imbalances, I decided to prescribe several Wisdom of the Earth essential oils for three months, and then re-test the three areas.

The parents were completely on board with me because they were facing a diagnosis of Asperger's Syndrome and the prescription drugs Cylert and Ritalin.

Raymond is a very spiritual person, and I used five drops of Spike Lavender on his feet during his first Craniosacral session. Within 10 minutes, he was asleep on the table and seemed to respond favorably to this approach. He was recharging his depleted state.

For the first three weeks I prescribed the following essences:

1. Black Cumin to improve protein levels and strengthen the immune system: 10 drops orally at breakfast and lunch.

2. Patchouli and Bay Laurel Leaf to address the heavy metal toxicities. Bay Laurel also was used as a protector against entities and to give Raymond courage to make the changes needed to fulfill the role his soul was meant to have in this life. Because of his withdrawn speaking ability, I thought the Bay Laurel would help him open his throat chakra. For these two essences, I recommended three applications per day: five drops in the morning, after school, and before bed. Raymond received both of these essences on the soles of his feet or on his lower back.

3. Mexican Lime. Two applications per day of five drops in the morning and after school. This essence helped Raymond to be more attentive and lifted his spirits. He enjoyed receiving these essences on the soles of his feet.

4. Frankincense. One application per day: Five drops on the top of his head before bed. I sensed that Raymond had a past life during the period of Jesus and I thought it would help him connect to the healing consciousness of Jesus.

After three weeks, when Raymond returned for another Craniosacral session, his parents were thrilled to report changes. He was beginning to become interested in books, he had better focus, and he was becoming more talkative. But, his mom said, he was still pretty tired by the end of the day.

During this Craniosacral session, several essences were calling me to use them on Raymond. I applied three drops of Mugwort on the soles of his feet to help him move his energy and release his anxiety, four drops of Fir Balsam on his low back to tonify his adrenal glands and ground him, three drops of Highland Lavender on his heart to open his heart chakra, and three drops of Violet on his head to heal his birth trauma and help him open up his joy. At the end of the session, he seemed to be even calmer. A few days later, his father called saying that Raymond was showing more energy at the end of the day.

We continued with the same essences for home use, and I saw him three weeks later. Again his energy seemed more balanced. His mom said he was having difficulty sleeping, so I recommended an insomnia protocol: Vetiver, Spikenard, and Wild Chamomile (four drops each) were added to his treatment program. His mom applied these three essences to the top of his head (moved phrase) every other day before bed, and he skipped the Frankincense during this sleep application. Within a week, his mom sent me an email saying he was sleeping deeply through the night.

When I saw Raymond at week nine of this protocol, his parents said he was beginning to do his schoolwork and he was making friends at school. His teacher was amazed. During our Craniosacral session, the following essences called me: three drops of Ponderosa Pine on his low back to help him ground; three drops of Jade Cypress on his third eye to help him open his spiritual and physical vision, and three drops of Davana to help him connect to a deeper part of himself. I changed the home protocol for his last three weeks:

1. Black Cumin to improve his immune function: 10 drops orally at breakfast and lunch
2. Geranium to improve balance of his nervous system: five drops in the AM and PM
3. Violet to help him heal traumas from his past lives as well as the birth trauma from his present life: five drops in the AM and PM
4. Vetiver, Spikenard, and Wild Chamomile for better sleep: four drops each three times per week.

I cut some of his hair and sent it off to the lab and told his parents that I would re-test him at week twelve.

Results of the Re-tests

The Tissue Mineral Analysis showed large improvements in his carbohydrate metabolism (calcium-magnesium ratio), his adrenal function returned to normal (sodium-potassium ratio), his dietary absorption improved greatly (phosphorous levels were normal), and his high heavy-metal levels of lead, mercury, arsenic, and aluminum were completely gone.

Biofield analysis: In *figures 4 and 5*, Raymond's biofields have become filled in and are much smoother. In figure 6, Raymond's chakras are lined up along the midline which suggests a new coherence in his energy.

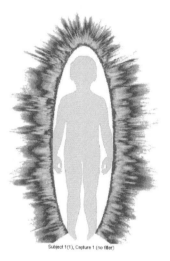

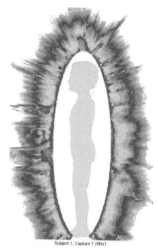

Robust Field After Essence Treatment
Figure 4

Robust Field after Twelve Week
Essence Protocol
Figure 5

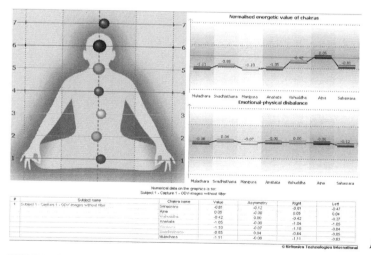

Figure 6

The essences have helped Raymond become more nourished and more connected to himself. His behavior is much calmer, and he is feeling joyous in his life.

I put him on a maintenance essence protocol to support his new energy:

1. Black Cumin to address his energy level and immune system: 10 drops orally at breakfast and lunch
2. Spike Lavender to reduce anxiety: five drops in the AM and PM on his heart chakra
3. Fir Needle Siberian Silver after school on his low back for grounding and adrenal support: five drops in the AM and PM
4. Vetiver, Spikenard, and Wild Chamomile: (four drops each) three times per week.

Developmental-Visual-Learning Assessment:
Raymond's developmental delays, sensory motor systems, primitive reflexes, and birth trauma all showed significant improvement. I prescribed some activities to help him integrate these brain-movement patterns and saw him again in three months to assess these motor skills. He is now thriving in school and sports!

❖ ❖ ❖ ❖ ❖ ❖ ❖

Final Thoughts

Quantum physicists like Fritz Albert Popp have shown we are made of photons. When we use subtle energy modalities to balance the biofield, we are able to improve incoherent energy patterns well before they show up in the physical body. Most allopathic medicine, with its focus on the molecular versus "quantum" level of health, treats disease with little connection to body-mind-spirit. Often patients are treated like machines. Pharmaceutical drugs contribute to our inability to connect to our biology for healing.

Using tools of quantum mechanics, however, we can look at the data from the body's own photons and electrons as a method to monitor wellness.

I foresee a new practitioner who can scan the field, perform electrodynamic tune-ups using subtle energies, create higher self alignments, and perform biophotonic balancing. This new practitioner will help us align with geocosmic fields, the biofields of the earth, and the cosmos. It is my hope that this paradigm helps guide our evolution to become a more loving, compassionate species that sees ourselves as part of the overall biodiversity on our planet.

I SENSE: AT PLAY IN THE FIELD OF HEALING

EPILOGUE

At this stage of our species' evolution, we are asked to recognize our authority at all levels of our lives. Our cellular structure is becoming more attuned to make changes not only on a molecular level, but also energetically. As we realize that the veils are becoming thinner between the material and spiritual worlds, our dreams can become part of our reality.

However, our deepest fears and anxieties may surface as we move to this new level of sensitivity. Know that experiencing these fears gives us an opportunity to invite them to die, so that more of our aliveness can be born.

As we continue to cycle through the birth-death-birth experience, a crystalline clarity will manifest that invokes a higher frequency within us. When we step into this new consciousness, a new simplicity will emerge. Using the pineal gland through the visual system to help us see from the inside out with great clarity and trust, we will finally realize:

We are the ambassadors of the New Earth.

I SENSE: AT PLAY IN THE FIELD OF HEALING

RESOURCES

Dr. Sam Berne
PO Box 458, Tesuque, NM 87574
505.469.4949
www.drsamberne.com/about
visionwellness@cybermesa.com

Workshops:
See www.drsamberne.com/events for a list of upcoming
workshops and registration information.

Books:
See www.newattention.net/books to order my previous books,
including:

- *Creating Your Personal Vision,* a mind-body guide for
  better eyesight, supporting self-healing to improve vision
  and reduce the need for eyeglasses
- *Without Ritalin: A Natural Approach to ADD,* a holistic
  approach for working with children diagnosed with
  hyperactivity disorders.
- *A.D.D. to Autism: Reaching Your Potential Naturally,*
  DVD offering complementary and holistic alternatives for
  helping children diagnosed within the spectrum of autism
  disorders.

Continuum Movement: For more information about this life-changing body-based modality that helps reconnect us to our inherent fluid nature, see www.continuummovement.com, or read founder Emilie Conrad's book, *Life on Land,* www.continuummovement.com/life-on-land.

Craniosacral Therapy: Learn more about this gentle hands-on therapy or find a practitioner in your area at: www.craniosacraltherapy.org.

The Dolphin Project: http://www.dolphinproject.org

Dr. Korotkov and the GDV camera: Learn more about Dr. Korotkov's work and the GDV camera at http://www.gdvsource.com/index.php and www.korotkov.org

Dr. Mary Milroy: www.GDVsource.com. Mary is the United States GDV distributor for KTI, the Russian-based company who manufactures the Electrophotonic imaging equipment. She is based in New Jersey.

Earth Island Institute: http://www.earthisland.org

Global Coherence Initiative: www.glcoherence.org, works to facilitate a shift in global consciousness to improve social harmony, environmental responsibility, and stewardship of our planet. This project is organized in part by Rollin McCraty, Ph.D., Executive Vice President and Director of Research at the Institute of HeartMath, www.heartmath.com.

Medicinal essential oils: I highly recommend the essences made by *Wisdom of the Earth.* Learn more from their website, www.wisdomoftheearth.com or from founder Barry Kapp's book Wisdom of the Earth Speaks, www.wisdomoftheearth.com/books.

Tresa Laferty: Learn more about animal communicator and aromatherapist Tresa Laferty and her business, Speak to the Earth, at www.speaktotheearth.com or contact her at tresa@tresalaferty.com or 262.902.2271.

Sacred Plant Medicine: *The Wisdom in Native American Herbalism* by Stephen Harrod Buhner. Order at www.gaianstudies.org/Bookstore, or learn more about Stephen's work at www.sacredplanttraditions.com/buhner.